MW01234115

OS/2 2.0
Quick Reference

Que Quick Reference Series

BARRY NANCE

OS/2 2.0 Quick Reference.

Copyright© 1992 by Que® Corporation.

Library of Congress Catalog No: 92-64361

ISBN: 1-56529-068-2

95 94 93 92   4 3 2 1

Interpretation of the printing code: the rightmost double-digit number is the year of the book's printing; the rightmost single-digit number, the number of the book's printing. For example, a printing code of 92-1 shows that the first printing of the book occurred in 1992.

This book is based on OS/2 2.0.

CREDITS

Publisher
Lloyd J. Short

Associate Publisher
Rick Ranucci

Acquisitions Editor
Tim Ryan

Product Director
Walter R. Bruce III

Production Editor
Colleen Totz

Technical Editor
Maria E. Tyne

Production Team
Claudia Bell, Michelle Cleary, Bob LaRoche,
Joy Dean Lee, Laurie Lee, Caroline Roop,
Linda Seifert, Sandra Shay

TRADEMARK ACKNOWLEDGMENTS

TABLE OF CONTENTS

INTRODUCTION

OS/2 2.0 Quick Reference describes the essential commands and procedures you need to use OS/2. The information is presented in an easy-to-look-up, handy format. This book is not intended to replace more comprehensive documentation. For more detailed instruction presented in a tutorial, narrative style, see Que's *Using OS/2 2.0*.

This book contains a command reference, a batch file programming guide, an Enhanced Editor reference, a guide to dealing with OS/2 messages, and an OS/2 survival guide. With *OS/2 2.0 Quick Reference*, you can look up an OS/2 command, a DOS command, a CONFIG.SYS statement, an Enhanced Editor procedure, or a particular error message quickly and easily.

Hints for Using This Book

Commands are a language you use to give instructions to OS/2 and DOS. A brief description follows the name of each command. Then you see up to four headings:

Syntax

Think of syntax as the grammar rules that tell how you can use each command. This book uses some simple conventions to make the syntax of each command clear and understandable.

For a command that operates on a file, the syntax information for the command shows:

_d:path_\filename.ext

In this command, **_d:_** represents a drive letter and **_path_**\ represents a single directory or a path of directories separated by backslashes (\). The portion in boldface italics, **_d:path_**\, is optional. The portion shown in boldface blue type, filename.ext, is required. After you type in each command, press Enter. Some commands are too long to fit on one line in this book; the continued lines are indented to indicate that they are part of the command.

> **NOTE:** If OS/2 cannot find the command you typed, the following message is displayed:
>
> ```
> The name specified is not recognized
> as an internal or external command,
> operable program, or batch file
> ```
>
> You can tell OS/2 where to find the command by modifying your PATH, as explained later in this section. You also can tell OS/2 where to find the command by prefixing the command with the drive letter and path (directory) containing that command. For example, type the following command:
>
> C:\OS2\CHKDSK
>
> This command tells OS/2 to look in the \OS2 directory on drive C for the CHKDSK command. OS/2 automatically sets up your PATH statement in the CONFIG.SYS file (for OS/2 sessions) and AUTOEXEC.BAT file (for DOS sessions) to point to all the directories containing your OS/2 and DOS commands. If OS/2 tells you that it cannot find a command, check your spelling of the command. You rarely if ever need to prefix a command with the drive letter and directory containing that command.

This command reference shows text that you type in uppercase letters. Any variable text you replace with text of your choosing appears in lowercase letters. As an example, look at the following syntax entry:

FORMAT d:

This command means that you must type the word FORMAT to format a disk. You replace d: with the drive letter of the disk you want to format.

Switches

Many commands have optional switches that modify how they work. Switches start with a slash. If you erase a group of files by typing DEL *.* /P, for example, the /P switch tells the DEL command to ask your permission before erasing each file.

Examples

Concrete examples offer the quickest, simplest way to see how a command works. You will find many examples in this section.

Note

You will find hints, background information, and—when appropriate—warnings in this section.

OS/2 2.0 COMMAND REFERENCE

The command reference explains how to use OS/2 and DOS commands in full-screen and windowed sessions. Commands appear in alphabetical order. You can use most of the commands in OS/2 or DOS sessions; those commands that you cannot use in both sessions are labelled *OS/2 Only* or *DOS Only*. The first section of the command reference describes commands you type at a DOS or OS/2 prompt; the second section explains the statements and commands you can insert into your CONFIG.SYS file.

ANSI

OS/2 Only

Enables you to run those OS/2 programs that require special support for the screen or keyboard. Most OS/2 programs do not require ANSI support.

Syntax

ANSI

ANSI ON

ANSI OFF

Examples

To find out whether ANSI support is available, type the following command and press Enter:

ANSI

To turn ANSI support off:

ANSI OFF

Note

This command affects only OS/2 sessions. The special support it provides is available in OS/2 sessions by default, but you can turn it off; very few programs require ANSI support. Similar support is available in DOS sessions only if you load the ANSI.SYS driver in CONFIG.SYS with a DEVICE statement.

APPEND

DOS Only

Tells DOS programs where to find data files.

Syntax

APPEND *dir1;dir2;...*

dir1 is a directory, such as C:\MEMOS.

dir2 is another directory.

... means that you can specify more directories. Separate them from each other with semicolons.

Examples

To tell DOS programs to look for data files in the
directories C:\ and D:\DATA:

APPEND C:\;D:\DATA

To find out where the current APPEND statement
tells DOS to look for data files:

APPEND

Notes

Data files that are in the current directory are
always available to a program, even if you do not
include the current directory in the APPEND statement. APPEND enables DOS programs to access files
in other directories you name, as though they were
in the current directory. They do not search other
directories if they find the files they need in the
current directory.

You normally use APPEND in AUTOEXEC.BAT, but
you also can type it in a DOS window. The list of
directories you specify with APPEND cannot be
more than 128 characters long.

APPEND works only in DOS sessions. The DPATH
command performs the same function in OS/2
sessions.

ASSIGN

DOS Only

Redirects requests for disk operations on one drive
to a different drive.

Syntax

ASSIGN *d1=d2*

d1 is the drive you specify.

d2 is the drive that DOS uses instead.

Do not type a colon after the drive letters.

Examples

To make DOS use drive C when you use a command
for drive A:

ASSIGN A=C

To cancel all previous drive assignments:

ASSIGN

Notes

Never use ASSIGN. It is obsolete. Instead of

ASSIGN A=C

use

SUBST A: C:\

A detailed discussion of the SUBST command
appears later in this command reference.

ATTRIB

Shows or changes a file's read-only and archive
attributes.

Syntax

ATTRIB +*A* -*A* +*R* -*R* d:\path\filename.ext /*S*

filename.ext specifies the file or files whose
attributes you want to change.

+*A* sets the archive flag, which means that the file
has not been backed up.

-A turns off the archive flag.

+R sets the read-only flag, which prevents the file from being changed or deleted.

-R turns off the read-only flag.

Switch

/S shows or changes attributes of files in subdirectories of filename.ext.

Examples

To make sure that your CONFIG.SYS file cannot be accidentally erased or changed:

ATTRIB +R \CONFIG.SYS

To turn off the archive flag on a temporary database file so that an incremental backup will skip the file as if it were already backed up:

ATTRIB -A \MYDATA.DBF

To find out which files in your \OS2 directory and all its subdirectories have not been backed up:

ATTRIB \OS2*.* /S

This command lists every file, with the letter A next to each one that has not been backed up.

To list every program file on a disk and its attributes:

ATTRIB *.EXE /S

Notes

Every file has several *attributes* (flags that store information about the file). OS/2 reserves most of the attributes for its own use but allows you to change the backup and read-only flags. Avoid turning off the read-only flag on OS/2's system files.

When you make an archival copy of a file with the BACKUP command, the archive flag is turned off. When you make an incremental backup later on, it includes only files whose archive flag is not set.

If you remember a file's name but cannot recall its location on a disk, use ATTRIB with the /S switch to find it.

BACKUP

OS/2 Only

Backs up a hard disk to floppy disks.

Syntax

> BACKUP *d1:dir\files* d2: /A /M /S
> */D:mm-dd-yy /T:hh:mm:ss /L:logfile*
> */F:size*

d1: is the hard disk you are backing up, such as C.

dir is the directory that you want to back up. The default is the root directory.

files specifies the files you want to back up. You can omit it if you want to back up all files in a directory.

You must specify at least one of *d1:*, *dir*, and *files*.

d2: is the letter of the floppy disk drive to which you are backing up, such as A.

Switches

/A adds files to an existing backup disk, leaving old backup files intact.

/M backs up only files that you created or changed since your last backup.

/S backs up files in subdirectories of *dir*.

/D:mm-dd-yy limits BACKUP to files created or changed since a given date.

/T:hh:mm:ss limits BACKUP to files created or changed since a given time. Use this switch only with the **/D** switch.

/L:logfile creates a log that lists the name of every file that is backed up. The log file tells which floppy disk contains each file so that you can restore a single file without rummaging through all the floppy disks. The default **logfile** is **d1:**\BACKUP.LOG.

/F:size formats floppy disks to the size you specify. Use this switch only if the floppy disks are not the default size for your drive. The following table shows the sizes you can choose.

Size	Description	Capacity
360	5 1/4-inch double density	360K
1200	5 1/4-inch high density	1.2M
720	3 1/2-inch double density	720K
1440	3 1/2-inch high density	1.44M
2880	3 1/2-inch ultra density	2.88M

Examples

To back up every file in every subdirectory on hard drive C to floppy disks in drive A and create a log file:

    BACKUP C: A: /S /L

To update a previous complete backup, adding only files that you created or modified since the last complete backup:

    BACKUP C: A: /A /M /S

To back up every file in C:\MEMOS that you
changed since noon on March 20, 1991:

BACKUP C:\MEMOS A: /D:3-20-91 /T:12:00

Notes

BACKUP may require a large number of floppy disks.
You should format them and discard any that have
bad sectors. BACKUP formats them if you do not; it
assumes that they are the default size for the drive
unless you specify a different size with the /F switch.
Write a number on each floppy disk because you
must insert them in order when you restore the
backup.

The files that BACKUP writes on floppy disks are not
immediately usable. To put the files back on your
hard disk, you must use the RESTORE command.

You cannot back up OS/2's system files. If you
restore a complete backup made with an earlier
version of OS/2, you will not crash the system by
writing over these critical files with obsolete
versions.

The COUNTRY statement in CONFIG.SYS determines
the national date and time format that the /D and /T
switches use.

BOOT

Loads a different operating system.

Syntax

BOOT /OS2

BOOT /DOS

Note

Use this command to switch between DOS and OS/2 if you installed them on drive C. Make sure that all programs have ended first so that you don't lose data.

CD or CHDIR

Shows or changes the current directory of a disk drive.

Syntax

CD *d1:*

CD *d1:*dir

d1: is the disk whose current directory you want to show or change. The default is the current disk.

dir is the directory to which you want to change.

Examples

To find out the name of the current drive and directory:

CD

To find out the name of the current directory of drive D:

CD D:

To move to the \OS2\MDOS directory on the current drive:

CD \OS2\MDOS

To move to the same directory as in the last example, if the current directory is C:\OS2:

CD MDOS

To move back to C:\OS2, if the current directory is
C:\OS2\MDOS:

CD ..

The double period is shorthand for the *parent*
directory, one level back from the current directory.

To move from C:\OS2\MDOS to C:\OS2\INSTALL:

CD ..\INSTALL

Notes

CD and CHDIR are different names for the same
command.

When you specify a drive *d1:*, you show or change
the name of that drive's current directory, but you
do not make *d1:* the current drive.

CHCP

Switches between national alphabets.

Syntax

CHCP *page*

page is the number of the code page for the alphabet you want to use.

Examples

To find out the number of the current code page:

CHCP

To switch to the multilingual codepage, assuming
that you loaded it in CODEPAGE and DEVINFO
statements in your CONFIG.SYS file:

CHCP 850

Notes

OS/2 stores many different national alphabets in *code pages*. You can load up to two pages through the CODEPAGE statement in CONFIG.SYS; only one page is active at a time. With CHCP, Change Code Page, you can choose either one. The number for each alphabet is in the on-line command reference, under the COUNTRY command.

If you work with people in other countries, they can read your files more easily if you use the multinational alphabet, code page 850. It includes most of the accented letters used in European languages. Stick to the letters A-Z and numerals 0-9 for file and directory names so that people in other countries can use them easily.

CHDIR

See CD.

CHKDSK

OS/2 Only

Analyzes a disk and gives you a report. Fixes disk problems.

Syntax

CHKDSK **d1:files** /F /V

d1: is the disk you want to analyze. The default is the current drive.

files specifies the files you want to analyze. CHKDSK checks whether each named file is stored all in one piece. The default is all files with no fragmentation report. To get the report and check all files, use *.*.

Switches

/**F** tells CHKDSK to fix any problems it finds.

/**V** displays the name and path of each file while CHKDSK checks it.

Examples

To analyze drive C:

CHKDSK C:

To analyze drive C and report any fragmented files:

CHKDSK C:*.*

To analyze drive C and repair any problems found:

CHKDSK C: /F

Notes

The files and directories on your hard disk can get scrambled if the power goes off while you are using your computer or if you turn your computer off without ending all applications first. Run CHKDSK from time to time to check for problems. You cannot CHKDSK a network drive.

CHKDSK reports useful statistics such as the number of files on a disk and the amount of free space. In DOS mode, it also gives a summary of memory usage. CHKDSK reports "bad sectors" if the sectors were marked as unusable when you formatted the disk. They are physically defective and cannot be repaired.

Ideally, a file's contents should be kept together in one place. Over time, however, the disk space becomes fragmented, and some files are spread over separate blocks. CHKDSK *.* tells you which files are fragmented. OS/2 still can work with them, but it will work more slowly.

CHKDSK may tell you it found chains of lost clusters.
These chains can be pieces of files that were
improperly saved, for example, because of a bug in
the program that created them. They also can be
files that a background program was writing when
you ran CHKDSK. You can rule that possibility out
by running CHKDSK alone with no background
sessions.

If the problem persists, run CHKDSK with the /F
option and answer Yes when it asks your permission
to fix the problem. CHKDSK collects every piece of
stray data that looks like it belongs to a file, and
puts each piece in a separate file in the root directory. It uses distinctive file names like FILE0000.CHK,
FILE0001.CHK, and so on. Inspect these file names
with the System Editor. Rename any files that look
like they contain data you still can use and then
delete the rest.

You cannot run CHKDSK /F on the drive from which
you booted OS/2. If you need to run it on your boot
disk, you must boot from drive A. Follow these steps
to boot from your original OS/2 floppy disk:

1. Shut down OS/2. Insert your original OS/2 Install disk in drive A. Hold down Ctrl and Alt at
   the same time, and press Del to reboot the
   computer.

2. When the install program prompts you, insert
   OS/2 disk 1. Press Enter when it asks whether
   you want to continue. When you see the
   Welcome to OS/2 screen, press Esc.

3. Insert a floppy disk that contains CHKDSK
   (disk 2 of the installation disks, or a separate
   disk to which you have copied CHKDSK.COM).
   Type:

   CHKDSK C:/F

4. Answer Yes when it asks your permission to
   repair the disk.

5. When CHKDSK finishes repairing the disk (but not before!), remove the floppy disk from drive A. Hold down Ctrl and Alt at the same time, and press Del to reboot the computer. Check for recovered files in your root directory.

CLS

Clears the screen.

Syntax

CLS

Note

OS/2 clears the screen and redisplays the command line prompt.

CMD

OS/2 Only

Starts a new copy of the OS/2 command processor, CMD.EXE.

Syntax

CMD */C /K command-line*

command-line is the program you want the command processor to run—an OS/2 command or a program with a CMD or EXE extension, plus any optional parameters.

Switches

/C terminates the new copy of CMD.EXE after it executes *command-line*.

/K keeps the new copy of CMD.EXE active after it executes *command-line*.

Example

To start a new copy of the OS/2 command processor CMD.EXE, use CMD to run the CHKDSK program, and then terminate CMD:

CMD /C CHKDSK

Note

If you use the /K switch, you can terminate the additional copy of CMD.EXE with the EXIT command.

COMMAND

Starts a new copy of the DOS command processor, COMMAND.COM.

Syntax

COMMAND */C /E:size /P command-line*

command-line is the program you want the command processor to run (a DOS command or a program with a BAT, COM, or EXE extension, plus any optional parameters). If you specify a *command-line*, you also must use the */C* switch.

Switches

/C passes ***command-line*** to COMMAND.COM. The new DOS command processor terminates after executing the command.

/E:size sets the size of the DOS environment in bytes. The default is 160 bytes, but you can set ***size*** to any higher value up to 32768. The size is rounded up to the next multiple of 16.

/P makes the new copy of COMMAND.COM permanent so that you cannot terminate it with the EXIT command. Use this switch only in the SHELL statement in your CONFIG.SYS file.

Examples

To start a new copy of the DOS command processor COMMAND, use COMMAND to run the CHKDSK program, then terminate COMMAND:

COMMAND /C CHKDSK

To start a copy of the DOS command processor, with an 800-byte environment, from a DOS or OS/2 window:

COMMAND /E:800

Use the EXIT command to close this new DOS session.

Note

You can use COMMAND /C inside a DOS batch file to run another batch file, but the DOS batch command CALL uses less memory to accomplish the same task.

COMP

Compares files.

Syntax

COMP *file1* *file2*

file1 and *file2* specify the two files, or sets of files, you want to compare.

Examples

To determine whether CONFIG.SYS and CONFIG.OLD are identical:

COMP CONFIG.SYS CONFIG.OLD

To determine whether C:\MYFILE and A:\MYFILE are identical:

COMP C:\MYFILE A:

To determine whether all the files on A exactly match files of the same names on C:

COMP A: C:

Notes

COMP reads the contents of two files and tells you whether they are identical. If they are not identical, it reports the first 10 characters that do not match. This report uses a hexadecimal format. After ten mismatches, COMP stops comparing.

Two files can be identical only if they are the same size. COMP tells you if they are not the same size and gives you the option to proceed anyway, up to the length of the shorter file.

If you do not specify either of the files to compare, COMP prompts you for the file names.

COPY (Combining Files)

Combines files.

Syntax

COPY file1+file2... target

file1 and file2 are the first two files you want to combine.

... means that you can specify more files. Separate them from each other with plus signs.

target is the name of the file that combines the contents of all source files.

Examples

To combine the contents of FILE1, FILE2, and FILE3 into a file called COMBINED:

COPY FILE1+FILE2+FILE3 COMBINED

To append the contents of FILE2 and FILE3 to FILE1:

COPY FILE1+FILE2+FILE3

Note

If you do not specify target, the contents of all the files are combined into file1.

COPY (Duplicating Files)

Copies files between disks or directories, optionally changing each file's name.

Syntax

> COPY files target

files specifies the files you want to duplicate.

target is the name or location of the duplicates you create.

Examples

To make a duplicate of MYFILE.TXT and name it MYCOPY.TXT:

> COPY MYFILE.TXT MYCOPY.TXT

To put a duplicate of MYFILE.TXT with the same name in the \DOCUMENT directory:

> COPY MYFILE.TXT \DOCUMENT

To copy all files with the extension TXT from the current directory to \DOCUMENT and change each file's extension to DOC:

> COPY *.TXT \DOCUMENT*.DOC

To copy every file in \MEMOS to a floppy disk in drive A:

> COPY \MEMOS*.* A:

To copy MYFILE.TXT to the printer:

> COPY MYFILE.TXT PRN

Notes

When you copy files to a different directory, first make sure that the directory exists. If a file that you tell COPY to create already exists, the old file is deleted first.

This command will not copy a file that is zero bytes long; you must use the XCOPY command.

DATE

Displays or sets the date.

Syntax

DATE *mm-dd-yy*

mm is the month (1-12).

dd is the day (1-31).

yy is the year (0-99, or 1900-1999).

Examples

To set the date to November 15, 1992:

DATE 11-15-92

To display the current date, and optionally change it:

DATE

Note

The computer remembers the date you set after you turn the power off. The COUNTRY command in CONFIG.SYS controls the way the date is formatted.

DEL or ERASE

Erases files.

Syntax

DEL files */P*

files specifies the files you want to erase.

Switch

/P asks your permission before deleting each file.

Examples

To erase the file PAYROLL.WK1 in the current directory:

DEL PAYROLL.WK1

To erase every file with the extension DOC in the \WORDPROC directory:

DEL \WORDPROC*.DOC

To modify the preceding example so that DEL displays each file name and asks your permission before erasing the file:

DEL \WORDPROC*.DOC /P

Notes

DEL will not erase OS/2's system files, or any files that you protected by setting their read-only attribute with the ATTRIB command. To erase directories, you must use the RD command.

Using DEL with wild cards can be dangerous. If you tell DEL to erase every file in a directory, it asks you to confirm the command. To see which files you will delete, use DIR with the same wild cards before you use DEL.

DETACH

OS/2 Only

Runs a program in the background.

Syntax

> DETACH command-line

command-line is the command you want to run in the background—an OS/2 command or a program with a CMD or EXE extension, plus any optional parameters.

Example

To format a floppy disk in the background:

> DETACH FORMAT A: /ONCE

Note

The command you run in the background must not require any input from the keyboard or mouse. You will not see anything the command tries to write to the screen. Because the command runs in the background, you can type other commands in that session without waiting for the first one to finish.

DIR

Lists the files in a directory.

Syntax

> DIR /F /N /P /W files

files specifies the directory or files you want to list.

Switches

/F lists files with full drive and path information, omitting date, time, and size.

/N lists files on a FAT drive in the format used for an HPFS drive.

/P lists files one screen at a time.

/W omits date, time, and size information, and lists file names across the screen so that more names will fit on-screen.

Examples

To list all files in the current directory of the current drive, showing each file's name, size in bytes, and date and time last modified:

DIR

To see the size, date, and time of \SALES\REGION1.WK1:

DIR \SALES\REGION1.WK1

To list only the names of all files with the extension SYS in the \OS2 directory, across the screen, one screen at a time:

DIR /P /W \OS2*.SYS

Note

DIR displays the volume label, directory name, number of files, and amount of space available on the drive unless you use the /F switch. The /F and /W switches do not work together.

DISKCOMP

Determines whether one floppy disk is an exact copy of another.

Syntax

DISKCOMP d1: d2:

d1: and **d2:** are the drives that hold the floppy disk to be compared. The command compares the disk

in **d1:** to the disk in **d2:**. You also can compare
floppy disks using only one drive.

Examples

To compare a floppy disk in drive A to one in
drive B:

DISKCOMP A: B:

To compare floppy disks by using only one drive:

DISKCOMP A: A:

Notes

DISKCOMP verifies the result of the DISKCOPY
command. It reports that two floppy disks are the
same only if one is an exact clone of the other, with
identical files in identical disk sectors. It ignores
floppy disk serial numbers because they are always
supposed to be different. To compare floppy disks
that were not copied with DISKCOPY, use the COMP
command.

DISKCOMP will not compare two floppy disks of
different sizes. You cannot use it to compare hard
disks, even if the hard disks are the same size.

High capacity floppy disks can be compared in
several passes if your computer does not have
enough memory available to hold their contents all
at once. If you are using a single drive, DISKCOMP
prompts you to swap the floppy disk when needed.

DISKCOPY

Duplicates a floppy disk.

Syntax

DISKCOPY d1: d2:

d1: is the drive that holds the floppy disk to be copied from.

d2: is the drive that holds the floppy disk to be copied to. You also can copy a floppy disk using only one drive.

Examples

To copy a floppy disk in drive A to one in drive B:

DISKCOPY A: B:

To copy a floppy disk using only one drive:

DISKCOPY A: A:

Notes

DISKCOPY makes an exact duplicate of a floppy disk. If you have not formatted the floppy disk to which you are copying, DISKCOPY formats it automatically. If DISKCOPY finds defects while formatting, it reports the problem but continues copying anyway. To verify that the copy is accurate, use the DISKCOMP command.

Because DISKCOPY makes an exact clone, it will not copy between two floppy disks of different sizes. You cannot use it to copy hard disks, even if they are the same size.

High capacity floppy disks are duplicated in several passes because your computer may not have enough memory to hold their contents all at once. If you are using a single drive, DISKCOPY prompts you to swap the floppy disk when needed.

Use DISKCOPY if you want to make a backup copy of your original OS/2 floppy disk.

DOSKEY

DOS Only

Controls command recall and editing.

Syntax

DOSKEY

Examples

To experiment with command recall, first type

DOSKEY

Next, list the contents of C:\OS2\MDOS:

DIR C:\OS2\MDOS

Press the up-arrow key once. The command is displayed again. Edit it by pressing Backspace eight times:

DIR C:\

Press Enter to execute the modified command, which now lists files in the root directory.

Notes

After you run DOSKEY, you can press the up arrow and down arrow to scroll through commands you previously typed. You can edit a recalled command and then execute it by pressing Enter.

DOSKEY works only in DOS sessions, but you can get the same effect in OS/2 sessions with the KEYS command.

ERASE

See DEL.

EXIT

Terminates the current command processor.

Syntax

EXIT

Note

If you loaded the current command processor from another one, you return to the original command processor; otherwise, you return to Presentation Manager.

FDISK and FDISKPM

OS/2 Only

Manages hard disk partitions.

Syntax

FDISK

FDISKPM

Notes

These commands set up partitions on your hard disk. Be careful when you use them. Changes you make to existing partitions erase data.

Before you can use a hard disk, you must partition it. Each partition looks like a separate drive. If you have one hard disk divided into two partitions, for example, your system probably shows two hard drives—C and D.

FDISKPM is a Presentation Manager version of FDISK. Except for the appearance of the interface, the two programs are identical. The on-line menus give complete instructions.

 FIND

OS/2 Only

Searches for text in files.

Syntax

FIND /C /N /V "text" file1 *file2...*

text is the string of characters for which you want to search.

file1 is a file you want to search for text.

file2 is another file you want to search.

... means that you can specify more files to search. Separate them from each other with blank spaces.

Switches

/C tells you how many lines contain text but does not display them.

/N displays each line that contains text and its line number.

/V displays all lines that do *not* contain text.

Examples

To show every line in CONFIG.SYS that contains the word "DEVICE":

FIND "DEVICE" C:\CONFIG.SYS

To show every line in CONFIG.SYS that contains the word "DEVICE" and the number of each line:

FIND /N "DEVICE" C:\CONFIG.SYS

To count how many lines in CONFIG.SYS contain the word "DEVICE" without showing each line:

FIND /C "DEVICE" C:\CONFIG.SYS

To show all lines in the files \BOOK\CHAPTER1.TXT and \BOOK\CHAPTER2.TXT that do *not* contain the lowercase letter *e*:

FIND /V "e" \BOOK\CHAPTER1.TXT
        \BOOK\CHAPTER2.TXT

Notes

The text you want to search for must be surrounded by double quotes. FIND detects only exact matches. Uppercase and lowercase are different. ("This" and "this" do not match.) You cannot find a phrase that is split between two lines.

You have to list the full name of each file you want to search. Wild cards do not work with FIND.

You can combine the /V switch with /C or /N, but you cannot use /C and /N together.

FORMAT

Prepares a disk for use and reports any defects.

Syntax

FORMAT d1: */ONCE /FS:file-system*
/L /V:label /F:size /4

d1: is the disk you want to format, such as A.

Switches

/ONCE formats one floppy disk. If you format a
floppy disk without this switch, FORMAT assumes
that you want to format another when you are
finished. You can answer No when it asks you to
insert another.

/FS:file-system tells which file system you want
OS/2 to use in that partition. */FS:HPFS* is the High
Performance File System. The default, */FS:FAT*, is
the DOS-compatible File Allocation Table format.
The */FS:* parameter is only valid for hard disks.

/L formats an IBM read-write optical disk.

/V:label specifies a volume label. If you do not use
/V, FORMAT asks you to type a label anyway.

/F:size tells OS/2 the capacity of the floppy disk you
are formatting. If the capacity of the disk is the
default for your drive, you do not need this switch;
otherwise, you must specify a value from the
following table.

Size	Description	Capacity
360	5 1/4-inch double density	360 KB
1200	5 1/4-inch high density	1.2 MB
720	3 1/2-inch double density	720 KB
1440	3 1/2-inch high density	1.44 MB
2880	3 1/2-inch ultra density	2.88 MB

/4 means the same thing as */F:360*—that you want to format a double density, 360K 5 1/2-inch floppy disk in a 1.2M drive. Floppy disks you format this way will not work reliably in lower-capacity drives.

Examples

To format a 1.44M floppy disk in a 1.44M drive A:

FORMAT A:

To format just one 720K floppy disk in a 1.44M drive A:

FORMAT A: /F:720 /ONCE

To format a 360K floppy disk in a 1.2M drive B:

FORMAT B: /4

or

FORMAT B: /F:360

To format hard drive D for the High Performance File System, and give it the label HPFSDRIVE:

FORMAT D: /FS:HPFS /V:HPFSDRIVE

Notes

FORMAT installs a file system on a disk and checks the surface for physical defects. If it finds defects, it locks the unusable sectors so that OS/2 will not place your data in them. You must format a disk before you can use it. If you reformat a disk that you have used before, all the data it holds is wiped out. You must partition a hard disk with FDISK before you can format it. You cannot format a network drive.

Most computers that can run OS/2 have high-capacity floppy disk drives. For best results, use high-density floppy disks in these drives. Never format a floppy disk to a higher capacity than it was designed for. Even if it works fine today, it may fail in six months or be unreadable on someone else's computer.

If you format a 360K floppy disk in a 1.2M drive, you should use it only in 1.2M drives; it will not work reliably in a 360K drive. 720K floppy disks formatted in a 1.44M drive with /F:720 work reliably in 1.44M or 720K drives, however.

GRAFTABL

DOS Only

Enables DOS programs to display line-drawing and national language characters on a CGA monitor in graphics mode.

Syntax

GRAFTABL nnn

nnn is the national language code page you want to use, or a question mark.

Examples

To enable DOS programs to display line-drawing characters in graphics mode, according to the U.S. code page:

GRAFTABL 437

To see what other code pages you can specify with this command:

GRAFTABL ?

Note

Use this command only if you have a CGA monitor.

HELP

Explains how to use a command, or what an error message means.

Syntax

HELP ON

HELP OFF

HELP *command-name*

command-name is the name of a DOS or OS/2 command.

HELP *message-number*

message-number is the number of an error message.

Examples

To see which keys you can press to switch between tasks, and how to use HELP:

HELP

To tell OS/2 or DOS to display at the top of the screen the keys you press to switch tasks:

HELP ON

To tell OS/2 or DOS not to display this information:

HELP OFF

To find out how to use the COPY command:

HELP COPY

To see an explanation of the OS/2 error message SYS0002:

HELP 2

Notes

Help on a command is available only for OS/2—not
for DOS.

When you ask for help on an OS/2 error message,
you do not have to type the letters SYS or the
leading zeros.

JOIN

DOS Only

Tells DOS to join a disk drive to a directory on
another drive.

Syntax

JOIN d1: d2:\dir

JOIN d1: /D

d1: is the drive you specify.

d2:\dir is the drive and directory that DOS uses
instead. The drives d1: and d2: must be different.

Switch

/D cancels any previous JOIN command for d1:.

Examples

To show all current JOINs:

JOIN

To tell DOS to treat drive A as the subdirectory
\DATA on drive C:

JOIN A: C:\DATA

To cancel the effect of the above JOIN command:

JOIN A: /D

Notes

If **directory-name** already exists, it must be empty. If it does not exist, it is created. It must be a sub-directory of the root directory—not of any other directory.

You can use JOIN to make old programs that run from a floppy drive run from a hard drive. Otherwise, avoid using this command. JOIN is dangerous to use with many programs, such as the commands CHKDSK, DISKCOMP, DISKCOPY, FORMAT, LABEL, and RECOVER.

KEYB

OS/2 Only

Tells the keyboard which national alphabet you want to use.

Syntax

KEYB nation *alternate*

nation is the country whose alphabet you want to use.

alternate is a number that selects an optional "enhanced" keyboard layout. It is available only if nation is Czechoslovakia, France, Italy, or the United Kingdom.

Examples

To switch to the Hungarian keyboard:

KEYB HU

To use the "enhanced" Czechoslovakian keyboard:

KEYB CS 245

Notes

Run this command only in a full-screen OS/2 session. It affects DOS full-screen sessions and all OS/2 sessions—windowed and full screen.

KEYB enables you to switch quickly to another national alphabet. It works only if you have a DEVINFO statement in CONFIG.SYS. To change the default keyboard layout permanently, modify the DEVINFO statement. The number for each alphabet is in the on-line command reference, under the COUNTRY command.

KEYS

OS/2 Only

Controls command recall and editing.

Syntax

KEYS ON

KEYS OFF

KEYS LIST

Examples

To turn command recall off:

KEYS OFF

To turn command recall on:

KEYS ON

To find out whether command recall is on:

> KEYS

To see which commands are available for recall:

> KEYS LIST

To experiment with command recall, first list the contents of C:\OS2:

> DIR C:\OS2

Press up arrow once. The command is displayed again. Edit it by pressing Backspace three times:

> DIR C:\

Press Enter to execute the modified command, which lists files in the root directory.

Notes

When KEYS is ON, you can scroll through commands you previously typed by pressing up arrow and down arrow. You can edit a recalled command and then execute it by pressing Enter.

DOSKEY works only in DOS sessions, but you can get the same effect in OS/2 sessions by using the KEYS command.

LABEL

Gives a name to a disk.

Syntax

> LABEL *d1:name*

d1: is the disk whose label you want to see or change, such as C. The default is the current drive.

name is what you want to call the disk—any combination of up to 11 letters and numerals.

Examples

To see the current drive's label, and optionally change it:

LABEL

To see the label of drive D, and optionally change it:

LABEL D:

To set the label of drive C to HARDDISK:

LABEL C:HARDDISK

Note

If you run the FORMAT command on a hard disk that has a label, it prompts you for the label and will not continue if you do not type it. This safeguard provides extra protection against formatting the hard disk by accident, which would destroy your data. You always should LABEL your hard disk.

LOADHIGH

DOS Only

Loads DOS memory-resident programs into upper memory.

Syntax

LOADHIGH path\program

path is the location of the memory-resident program.

program is the name of the memory-resident program. Follow it with any arguments you would use if you typed it at the command line.

Example

To load APPEND into upper memory, with C:\OS2 and C:\OS2\SYSTEM as arguments:

LOADHIGH APPEND C:\OS2;
C:\OS2\SYSTEM

Note

Memory-resident programs, also known as TSRs, are DOS commands and applications that run in the background. If you load TSRs in upper memory, you leave more lower memory free for other programs.

MAKEINI

OS/2 Only

Recovers from a Corrupt OS2.INI error.

Notes

Use this command only if you receive an error message that says your OS2.INI or OS2SYS.INI file is corrupt, or if OS/2 fails to boot. Those files hold vital information that OS/2 needs to run on your computer. If they become damaged, follow these steps to re-create them:

1. Shut down OS/2. Insert your original OS/2 Install disk in drive A. Hold down Ctrl and Alt at the same time, and press Del to reboot the computer.

2. When the install program asks you, insert OS/2 disk 1. Press Enter when it asks whether you want to continue. When you see the Welcome to OS/2 screen, press Esc.

3. Type the following commands exactly as shown:

   C:

   CD\OS2

   DEL OS2.INI

   MAKEINI OS2.INI INI.RC

   DEL OS2SYS.INI

   MAKEINI OS2SYS.INI INISYS.RC

4. Remove the floppy disk from drive A. Hold down Ctrl and Alt at the same time, and press Del to reboot the computer. The repair procedure is completed.

MD or MKDIR

Creates a directory.

Syntax

   MD *d1:path*\dir

d1: is the disk where you want to create the new directory. The default is the current disk.

path is the parent of the new directory. The default is the current directory.

dir is the name of the new directory you want to create.

Examples

To make a directory \WORDPROC in the root directory:

   MD \WORDPROC

To make a directory \MEMOS as a subdirectory of an existing directory \WORDPROC on drive D:

MD D:\WORDPROC\MEMOS

To make a directory \STUFF as a subdirectory of the current directory:

MD STUFF

Note

You cannot create a directory with the same name as a file that already exists in the same location.

MEM

DOS Only

Displays the amount of available memory in a DOS session.

Syntax

MEM

Note

This command tells how much conventional, expanded (EMS), and extended (XMS) memory is available for DOS programs.

MODE (Communications)

Controls the communications port.

Syntax

MODE COMx:*rate,parity,databits,stopbits,P*

COMx is a communications port, such as COM1 or COM2.

rate is bits per second. The default is 1200. You do not have to type the last two zeros of *rate*. For example, 12 is the same as 1200.

parity is a single character that tells OS/2 how to verify that data is sent correctly. Use N for none, O for odd, E for even, M for mark, or S for space parity. E is the default.

databits is the number of bits used to represent one character. You can use 5, 6, 7, or 8. The default is 7.

stopbits is the number of bits added to mark the end of each character. You can use 1, 1.5, or 2. The default generally is 1.

P tells DOS to wait up to 30 seconds for the port to respond. *P* is available in DOS sessions only.

Examples

To see the current settings for the second communications port:

    MODE COM2

To set up the first communications port for 2400 bits per second, even parity, seven databits, and one stopbit:

    MODE COM1:2400,E,7,1

Notes

You must load support for communications ports by including COM.SYS in your CONFIG.SYS file before you use MODE to configure the ports.

You can leave out any item you do not want to change, but you must include the comma that would have followed that item (unless the item is the last one you want to change). To change to eight data-bits while leaving all previous settings alone, for example, type the following:

MODE COM1:,,8

The *P* option, available only in a DOS session, tells the system to wait up to 30 seconds for the port to respond, which is useful if you have a serial printer that may be busy.

MODE (Printer)

OS/2 Only

Controls a parallel printer.

Syntax

MODE LPTx *width,spacing,P*

LPTx tells OS/2 which printer to set up. The printer can be LPT1, LPT2, or LPT3. You can use PRN as another name for LPT1.

width tells OS/2 how many characters to print on one line. The width can be 80 or 132.

spacing tells OS/2 how many lines to print per inch. Spacing can be 8 or 6.

P tells OS/2 to keep trying to send each line until the printer responds. If you do not specify P and the printer is busy, OS/2 displays an error message.

Examples

To tell the first parallel printer to put 132 characters on a line and print 8 lines per inch:

MODE LPT1 132,8

You can leave out any item you do not want to change, but you must include the comma that would have followed that item (unless the item is the last one you want to change). To tell the third parallel printer to keep trying to send each line until the printer responds without changing the width or spacing, for example, type the following:

MODE LPT3 ,,P

Note

This command works only on parallel printers.

MODE (Screen)

OS/2 Only

Controls the screen mode.

Syntax

MODE *CONx mode,lines*

CONx tells OS/2 which physical display to use, if your computer has two monitors. The first is CON1 and the second is CON2. You do not need to use this parameter if you have only one monitor.

mode specifies the kind of monitor you have. MONO indicates a monochrome (black and white) display, and CO80 indicates a color monitor that can show 80 text columns.

lines is the number of lines to display on-screen. Choose 25, 43, or 50. The default is 25.

Examples

To show 50 lines on the screen:

MODE MONO,50

To show 43 lines on your second monitor:

MODE CON2 MONO,43

Note

This command works only for full-screen OS/2 sessions.

Displays a file one screen at a time.

Syntax

MORE< file

file is the file you want to view.

Example

To see \CONFIG.SYS one screen at a time:

MORE< \CONFIG.SYS

Notes

Think of the less-than sign as part of the command's name. You need to include it because MORE is a special type of program known as a *filter*. Filters are an advanced topic that this book does not cover.

MORE displays the file's contents one screen at a time. Press Enter when you want to go on to the next screen. If you do not want to see the rest of the file, press Ctrl-C.

MOVE

Moves files from one directory to another on the
same drive.

Syntax

> MOVE files target

files specifies the files you want to move.

target is the new location for the files.

Examples

To remove all files with the extension DOC from the
root directory and put them in \DOCUMENT:

> MOVE *.DOC \DOCUMENT

To modify the last example so that the extension of
each file is changed to TXT:

> MOVE *.DOC \DOCUMENT*.TXT

To transfer OLDFILE.A from the current directory to
\DATA, rename it as NEWFILE.B, and delete the
original:

> MOVE OLDFILE.A \DATA\NEWFILE.B

To remove the \DOCUMENT directory, and any
subdirectories and files it contains, and re-create
it as a subdirectory of an existing directory
\WORDPROC:

> MOVE \DOCUMENT \WORDPROC

To rename the \DOCUMENT directory as \DOC,
assuming that no \DOC directory already exists:

> MOVE \DOCUMENT \DOC

Note

MOVE combines the functions of the COPY, RENAME, RD, MD, and DEL commands. MOVE removes files from one directory and adds the files to the other directory.

PRINT

Prints files.

Syntax

> PRINT file1 *file2... /D:LPTx*
>
> PRINT /C
>
> PRINT /T

file1 and *file2* are files you want to print.

... means that you can specify more files to print. Separate them from each other with blank spaces. You also can use wild cards.

Switches

/D:LPTx tells OS/2 which printer to use. The first three printers are LPT1, LPT2, and LPT3; network printers can have higher numbers. The default is LPT1.

/C cancels the file that is currently printing. OS/2 still prints any other files you sent to the printer.

/T cancels all files you sent to the printer.

—

Examples

To send the file \MAIL\LETTER1.TXT to the second printer:

> PRINT \MAIL\LETTER1.TXT /D:LPT2

To print the files LETTER1.TXT and LETTER2.TXT in your \MAIL directory:

> PRINT \MAIL\LETTER1.TXT
> \MAIL\LETTER2.TXT

To print all TXT files in the \MAIL directory whose names begin with LETTER:

> PRINT \MAIL\LETTER*.TXT

Notes

PRINT works only with plain text files. If you PRINT a word processing document, you probably will not get the results you want because most word processors put nonprinting and special control characters in a document file. If you tell your word processor to save a file as plain text, however, you can PRINT the document.

You cannot use the /C or /T switch with a file name.

PROMPT

Sets the string of characters that is displayed at the command line.

Syntax

> PROMPT *string*

string is a series of characters to display. You can use most characters that you can type from the keyboard and any of the following special codes:

Code	Meaning
$$	$
$_	new line
$a	&
$b		
$c	(
$d	date
$e	"escape" character
$f	)
$g	>
$h	backspace
$i	help information
$l	<
$n	current drive
$p	current drive and directory
$q	=
$s	space
$t	time
$v	version of the operating system

Examples

To set the prompt to show the current date and time on one line, and the current drive and directory on the next:

> PROMPT Date$q$d$sTime$qt_$p

To restore the default prompt:

> PROMPT

Note

The default prompt in an OS/2 session is help information plus current drive and directory. In a DOS session, the default prompt is current drive, directory, and an angle bracket. The system stores the prompt as a string of characters in the environment. You can display it with the SET command.

RD or RMDIR

Removes a directory.

Syntax

> RD *d1:path*\dir

d1: is the disk from which you want to remove a directory. The default is the current disk.

path is the parent of the directory to remove. The default is the current directory.

dir is the name of the directory you want to remove.

Examples

To remove the directory \WORDPROC\LETTERS from drive D:

> RD D:\WORDPROC\LETTERS

To remove the directory \WORDPROC\LETTERS, if \WORDPROC is the current directory:

> RD LETTERS

Note

You can remove only an empty directory (a directory that contains no files and no subdirectories). You cannot remove the current directory or the root directory.

RECOVER

Partially salvages files from a disk with bad sectors.

Syntax

RECOVER *files*

files specifies which files you want to salvage. You cannot use wild cards.

Examples

To salvage A:\MYFILE.TXT, placing whatever can be saved in the root directory with a name like FILE0000.REC, and then delete the original file:

RECOVER A:\MYFILE.TXT

To wipe out the entire directory structure of a floppy disk in drive A:

RECOVER A:

Notes

This command attempts to read all the data in a file and places it in a new file in the root directory with a name like FILE0000.REC or FILE0001.REC. If it cannot read the data in a particular sector, it substitutes zeros. It then deletes the original file. If the file is a program, the program is unlikely to work because part of the code was replaced by zeros.

Use RECOVER as a last resort, and only on files that you know are unreadable. Always specify a file; if you specify a disk or directory, the command recovers all the files the disk or directory contains. The root directory can hold only a limited number of files, and if you try to RECOVER too many files at once, some may be lost. If you RECOVER a good file, it will move the file to the root directory and give the file an unrecognizable name. For safety, RE-COVER does not work on a network drive.

REN or RENAME

Changes a file's name.

Syntax

REN oldname newname

oldname is the file's original name.

newname is the name you want to give it instead.

Examples

To change the name of a file in the \PLANS directory on drive C from NEWPLAN.DOC to OLDPLAN.DOC:

REN C:\PLANS\NEWPLAN.DOC
OLDPLAN.DOC

To change the name of JULIET1.DAT, JULIET2.DAT, and so on, to ROMEO1.TXT, ROMEO2.TXT, and so on:

REN JULIET*.DAT ROMEO*.TXT

Note

You can specify a drive and path only for oldname. REN uses the same drive and path for newname, and it will not work if a file called newname already exists there. It cannot change a subdirectory's name.

REPLACE

Selectively copies files.

Syntax

REPLACE files target /A /F /P /R /S /U /W

files specifies the files you want to copy.

target tells the location to which you want to copy them. The default is the current drive and path.

Switches

/A restricts the command to files that do not exist on target.

/F makes the command fail if you try to copy a file with OS/2 extended attributes to a drive that does not support them.

/P asks your permission before adding or replacing each file.

/R enables REPLACE to write over read-only files.

/S replaces files in all subdirectories of target.

/U replaces files only with newer versions.

/W waits for you to insert a floppy disk. Use /W when you need to swap floppy disks.

Examples

To copy all files from C that do not already exist on A:

REPLACE A:*.* C: /A

To replace files in every directory of C with files of the same name from A:

REPLACE A:*.* C: /S

To replace every file on drive C named FINAL.TXT
with the one in your \ULTIMATE directory:

REPLACE C:\ULTIMATE\FINAL.TXT C: /S

Note

You cannot use the /A switch with /S or /U. You
cannot REPLACE OS/2's critical system files or any
hidden files.

RESTORE

OS/2 Only

Retrieves files from a backup.

Syntax

RESTORE d1: d2:*files* /S /N /M /P
/A:*yy-mm-dd* /L:*hh:mm:ss* /B:*yy-mm-dd*
/E:*hh:mm:ss*

d1: is the drive that holds the backup floppy disk
you want to restore.

d2: is the hard drive to which you want to restore
the backed up files.

files specifies the directory and files you want to
restore. To do a complete restore, omit ***files*** and
use the /S switch.

Switches

/S restores files in all subdirectories. If you do not
use /S, only files in the directory you specify are
restored.

/N restores only files that do not exist on the hard
drive (if you deleted them since making the backup,
for example).

/M ignores files that you have not modified since you made the backup. Only files that you deleted or changed since then are restored. Use */M* if you made accidental changes to your files and want to restore them to the way they were before you changed them.

/P asks your permission before replacing any file that you changed since you backed it up. This switch protects against accidentally wiping out the changes you made since the backup.

/A:yy-mm-dd and */L:hh:mm:ss* tell RESTORE to undo changes you made *after* a given date and time. Use */L* only with */A*.

/B:yy-mm-dd and */E:hh:mm:ss* tell RESTORE to undo changes you made *before* a given date and time. Use */E* only with */B*.

Examples

To restore all the files from the backup floppy disk in drive A to drive C:

RESTORE A: C: /S

To restore all backed up files you modified since 6:00 p.m. on March 1, 1991:

RESTORE A: C: /S /A:3-1-91 /L:18:00

To restore all Lotus worksheets in C:\123G:

RESTORE A: C:\123G*.WK*

Note

This command restores files from a floppy disk backup you made with the BACKUP command. Because BACKUP wrote these files in a special format, commands like COPY cannot work with them; only BACKUP and RESTORE can work with these files. If the backup contains more than one floppy disk, RESTORE prompts you to insert the floppy disks in the right order.

You only can restore files to the same directory they were in when you backed them up. If the directory no longer exists, RESTORE creates it. You cannot restore files that OS/2 locked because they are in use (files used by programs that are running in the background, for example). Because BACKUP will not copy OS/2's most critical system files, you cannot use RESTORE to create a bootable disk.

The COUNTRY statement in CONFIG.SYS governs the national date and time format that the */A*, */B*, */E*, and */L* switches use.

You cannot restore a backup made with any DOS version earlier than 3.3.

RMDIR

See RD.

SORT

Sorts the lines in a file alphabetically.

Syntax

SORT <input-file >output-file */R /+n*

input-file is the file that you want to sort.

output-file is the name of the sorted file.

Switches

/R sorts in reverse alphabetical order.

/+n starts the sort in column number *n*. The default is the first column.

Examples

Suppose that you have a mailing list in ADDRESS.DAT that lists your customers' names in the first 20 columns, street addresses in the next 30 columns, and cities in the next 10 columns. These examples will sort it in various ways and put the sorted output in SORTED.DAT.

To sort by customer name:

SORT <ADDRESS.DAT >SORTED.DAT

To sort ADDRESS.DAT by street address, which begins in column 21:

SORT <ADDRESS.DAT >SORTED.DAT /+21

To sort ADDRESS.DAT in reverse order by city, which begins in column 51:

SORT <ADDRESS.DAT >SORTED.DAT /+51 /R

Notes

SORT works only on files up to 64,000 bytes long. The input and output files must have different names; the original file is not replaced with the sorted version.

Files are sorted according to the alphabet of the country you specify with the COUNTRY command. Upper- and lowercase letters are equivalent, and numerals come before letters.

SPOOL

Redirects a file that you send to one printer so that it prints on a different printer.

Syntax

SPOOL /D:printer1 /O:printer2

Switches

/D:printer1 is the printer to which you send a file. This printer can be any parallel printer such as PRN or LPT1 but not a serial printer such as COM1.

/O:printer2 is the printer to which the file really goes. This printer can be any parallel printer such as PRN or LPT1, or any serial printer such as COM1.

Examples

To make any file you send to PRN come out on a serial printer on COM1 instead:

SPOOL /D:PRN /O:COM1

To cancel any SPOOL command that redirects LPT2 to another printer:

SPOOL /D:LPT2 /O:LPT2

Note

You must install COM.SYS in your CONFIG.SYS file before you use the SPOOL command to direct files to a serial printer.

START

OS/2 Only

Runs a program automatically.

Syntax

START *"title"* /C /K /N /B /F /PGM /FS /PM
/WIN /DOS /MAX /MIN /I command-line

"title" is the name that appears at the top of the program's window. *"title"* can be up to sixty characters and must be in double quotes.

command-line is the program's name plus any parameters it needs.

Switches

/C closes the window after the program terminates.

/K keeps the window open after the program terminates.

/N runs the program directly without loading the OS/2 command processor CMD.EXE. The program must have an EXE extension.

/B runs the program in a background window.

/F runs the program in a foreground window.

/PGM indicates that *command-line* is enclosed in double quotes.

/FS runs the program in a full-screen session.

/PM runs the program in a Presentation Manager window.

/WIN runs the program in a window.

/DOS runs a *bound* program (a program that can run under DOS or OS/2) in a DOS window.

/MAX maximizes the window.

/MIN minimizes the window (makes it an icon).

/I enables the program to use the global environment instead of giving the program its own environment.

Examples

To open a windowed DOS session:

    START /WIN /DOS

To copy all the files from a floppy disk to your hard disk in a background window:

> START "Copy files" /B COPY A:*.*
>   C:\path*.*

To run the OS/2 program C:\WP\WORDPROC.EXE and load the file MEMO.TXT in a maximized, foreground Presentation Manager window named "WP" that will close when you exit the program:

> START "WP" /C /F /MAX C:\WP\WORDPROC
>   MEMO.TXT

Note

You normally use START in the STARTUP.CMD file that runs every time you turn the computer on. You can use it to load the programs you run every time you use your computer.

SUBST

DOS Only

Establishes an alias consisting of a drive letter for a path. You then can use the drive letter to refer to a long path instead of typing the path.

Syntax

> SUBST d1: d2:\dir
>
> SUBST d1: /D

d1: is the drive you specify in a DOS command.

d2:\dir is the drive and subdirectory that DOS uses instead.

Switch

/D cancels any previous SUBST command for d1:.

Examples

To show all current drive substitutions:

SUBST

To tell DOS to treat the directory \DATA on drive C as though it were a separate drive Z and then list the files in that directory:

SUBST Z: C:\DATA

DIR Z:

To cancel the effect of the above SUBST command:

SUBST Z: /D

Notes

If you already have a drive d1:, it becomes unavailable while the SUBST command is in effect.

SUBST enables you to run from a hard drive old programs that normally run from a floppy drive. Do not use the following commands on a substituted path: CHKDSK, DISKCOMP, DISKCOPY, FORMAT, LABEL, and RECOVER.

TIME

Displays or sets the time.

Syntax

TIME *hh:mm:ss.xx*

hh is hours (0-23).

mm is minutes (0-59).

ss is seconds (0-59).

xx is hundredths of a second (0-99).

Examples

To set the time to 5.98 seconds after 8:21 p.m.:

TIME 20:21:5.98

To set the time to midnight:

TIME 0

To display the current time, and optionally change it:

TIME

Note

You must use the 24-hour clock. The computer remembers the time you set after you turn the power off. The COUNTRY command in CONFIG.SYS controls the way the time is formatted.

TREE

Displays all directories on a disk.

Syntax

TREE *d1: /F*

d1: is the drive whose directory structure you want to display. The default is the current drive.

Switch

/F lists the name of every file in each directory.

Examples

To list all the directories on the default drive:

TREE C:

To list all the directories on drive C and all the files in each directory:

TREE C: /F

TYPE

Displays a file on-screen.

Syntax

TYPE file

file specifies the file you want to display.

Example

To show the contents of \CONFIG.SYS on-screen:

TYPE \CONFIG.SYS

Note

If the file is too long to fit on one screen, it scrolls by too rapidly to read. Use the MORE command to display the file one screen at a time.

UNDELETE

Restores a file you recently erased.

Syntax

UNDELETE *dir\files* /A /F /S /L

dir is the directory you want to back up.

files specifies the files you want to back up.

If you do not specify *dir* or *files*, UNDELETE searches for all deleted files in the current directory.

Switches

/A restores every deleted file in the directory.

/F erases files completely so that no one can recover them.

/L lists the files that can be restored but does not actually restore them.

/S restores every deleted file in *dir* and in all its subdirectories.

Examples

To display the names of the deleted files in the current directory that can be restored:

UNDELETE /L

To erase your performance appraisal in C:\PERSONAL\REVIEW.DOC so that no one can recover it:

UNDELETE C:\PERSONAL\REVIEW.DOC /F

Note

When you delete a file, OS/2 moves the file's data to a hidden area on your hard disk. The deleted file is intact, but its sectors are candidates for reuse as you write new files. UNDELETE enables you to resurrect a deleted file if you act before OS/2 uses that file's disk sectors to store new files. The area for deleted files is limited in size. When this area fills up, OS/2 discards the oldest files to make room for new ones.

UNPACK

Restores compressed files on an OS/2 installation floppy disk to their normal, uncompressed form. Performs a selective installation of a specific file.

Syntax

UNPACK packed-file target /N:*filename*

UNPACK packed-file /SHOW

packed-file is the name of the compressed file.

target is the drive and directory to which you want to copy the unpacked file.

Switches

/N:*filename* specifies the name of a file that you want to extract from a bundle that contains more than one file.

/SHOW displays the names of the files combined in a packed bundle (filename BUNDLE on an installation disk).

Examples

To extract XCOPY.EXE from the installation floppy disk in drive A and write it to the \OS2 directory on drive C:

UNPACK A:XCOPY.EXE C:\OS2

To display the names of the files packed into the bundle GROUP.DA@ on drive A:

UNPACK A:GROUP.DA@ /SHOW

To extract FORMAT.COM from the floppy disk file
BUNDLE.DA@ that contains it and put the extracted
file in C:\OS2:

> UNPACK A: BUNDLE C:\OS2
> /N:FORMAT.COM

Notes

Many of the files on the OS/2 distribution floppy
disk are compressed so that they take up less room.
OS/2 occupies fewer floppy disks this way. The
installation program automatically unpacks them.
If you accidentally lose one of OS/2's files but know
which disk contains that file, you can unpack it
yourself, which is often easier than reinstalling OS/2.

You can display the names of the files that are
combined in a packed bundle (file name BUNDLE)
by running UNPACK with the /SHOW option.

VER

Displays the version of OS/2 you are using.

Syntax

> VER

Example

To display which OS/2 version is running:

> VER

If you are using OS/2 2.0, the system responds:

```
The Operating System/2 Version
is 2.00
```

VERIFY

Checks that data is written to a disk.

Syntax

VERIFY ON

VERIFY OFF

Note

If VERIFY is ON, OS/2 confirms that *something* was written to the disk, but it does not guarantee that the intended data reached the surface of the disk. This is not worth the extra time OS/2 requires to confirm this information. You should leave VERIFY OFF.

VIEW

OS/2 Only

Looks up a topic in an on-line help document.

Syntax

VIEW book *topic*

book is a help file with the extension INF.

topic is the subject you want to look up.

Examples

To look up the VIEW command in the on-line command reference:

VIEW C:\OS2\BOOK\CMDREF VIEW

To find out how the REXX language uses loops:

VIEW C:\OS2\BOOK\REXX LOOPS

Notes

OS/2 comes with two help files in its BOOK directory. Some applications add their own help files.

You also can use the HELP command to look up a
topic. The following two lines are equivalent to the
VIEW examples above:

HELP VIEW

HELP REXX LOOPS

If you do not specify book, HELP assumes that you
mean CMDREF. With VIEW, you always must type
the name of the help file without the INF extension
to access other help besides that from CMDREF.

VOL

Displays a disk's label and serial number.

Syntax

VOL d1:

d1: is the drive whose label you want to examine.
The default is the current drive.

Examples

To display the label of the current drive:

VOL

To display the label of drive C:

VOL C:

Notes

Every disk formatted by OS/2 (and by later versions of DOS) has a serial number assigned by the system. You also should give the disk a label, which can be any combination of up to 11 letters and numbers. The VOL command displays the serial number and the label.

If you run the FORMAT command on a hard disk that has a label, it prompts you for the label and does not continue until you type it, which provides extra protection against accidentally formatting the hard disk.

OS/2 uses the serial number to keep track of your floppy disk. If a program is writing to a floppy disk, and you change the floppy disk before it finishes, the system can detect the change by comparing the serial numbers.

XCOPY

Selectively copies files, by date or other criteria, including files in subdirectories underneath a directory.

Syntax

XCOPY dir *target* /S /E /D:mm-dd-yy

dir specifies the directory you want to duplicate.

target is the location of the duplicate you create. If you do not specify a drive and directory, XCOPY uses the current drive and directory.

Switches

/S copies files in dir and all its subdirectories.

You can use */E* with */S* to copy subdirectories even if they contain no files.

/D:mm-dd-yy copies only files created or changed since a given date.

Examples

To copy every file in the \MEMOS directory of drive C to a disk in drive A:

    XCOPY C:\MEMOS A:

To copy \MEMOS directory of drive C and every subdirectory of \MEMOS—whether or not it contains any files—to floppy drive A:

    XCOPY C:\MEMOS A: /S /E

CONFIG.SYS COMMANDS

ANSI

DOS Only

Enables you to run the rare DOS program that requires special support for the screen or keyboard.

Syntax

    DEVICE=path\ANSI.SYS */L*

path is the location of the file ANSI.SYS. By default, path C:\OS2\MDOS.

/L prevents applications from overriding the number of rows you have set on-screen.

Example

To load special screen and keyboard support, and enable applications to set the number of rows on-screen, type the following in CONFIG.SYS:

DEVICE=\OS2\MDOS\ANSI.SYS

Note

This command affects only DOS sessions. The special support it provides is available in OS/2 sessions by default, but you can turn it off with the OS/2 ANSI command. Very few programs require it.

AUTOFAIL

OS/2 Only

Gives you a choice in dealing with certain hardware errors.

Syntax

AUTOFAIL=YES

AUTOFAIL=NO

Notes

Suppose that you run an application that uses a file on a floppy disk, but you forget to insert the disk. If you have AUTOFAIL=NO in your CONFIG.SYS file, OS/2 displays a dialog box describing the problem and asks you to choose an Abort, Retry, or Fail action. In this case, you would want to insert the disk and then tell OS/2 to try again to give the file to the application.

If you set AUTOFAIL=NO, OS/2 tells your application software that the file is unreadable without giving you a chance to correct the problem. The recommended setting is OFF.

BREAK

DOS Only

Controls how quickly DOS programs stop when you interrupt them by pressing Ctrl-Break.

Syntax

BREAK=ON

BREAK=OFF

Notes

You can stop many DOS programs by holding down Ctrl and pressing Break. When BREAK is OFF, DOS stops the program the next time it tries to read a character from the keyboard or to write to the screen or a printer. If you set BREAK=ON in your CONFIG.SYS file, DOS checks for Ctrl-Break more frequently but runs your programs more slowly.

BREAK is OFF by default. You should leave this setting OFF unless you have problems interrupting programs with Ctrl-Break.

BUFFERS

Sets aside a part of memory that OS/2 uses to hold disk data.

Syntax

BUFFERS=n

n is a number in the range of 1 to 100 that tells how many disk buffers you want to use. Each buffer takes up to 512 bytes.

Notes

When data moves to or from a disk drive, it flows through a special area of memory called a buffer. When you use many different files at once, your system runs faster if each file has its own buffer. Each buffer takes up a small amount of memory, however, leaving a little less memory to run your programs.

The default, BUFFERS=30, usually works well. If you have plenty of memory and want to use some of it to speed up disk operations, increase the size of your disk cache (using the CACHE and DISKCACHE commands) instead of setting more BUFFERS.

CACHE

DOS Only

Makes your hard disk seem faster by keeping the data you use most frequently in memory.

Syntax

RUN=C:\OS2\CACHE.EXE */LAZY:status*
/MAXAGE:time

status is ON if lazy writes are enabled and OFF if they are not enabled. If *status* is ON, the cache delays writing data to the disk when the system is busy.

time is the maximum length of time data can stay in the cache before OS/2 writes it to the disk. The time is measured in thousandths of a second; the default value, 5000, means 5 seconds.

Example

To set up a disk cache every time you boot OS/2, insert the following line in CONFIG.SYS:

```
RUN=C:\OS2\CACHE.EXE /LAZY:ON
```

Notes

If you use only a few programs and files at a time, you read the same parts of your hard disk over and over. A disk cache saves what you have most recently read in memory and reads it directly from memory when you need it again. It can make your hard disk seem much faster because memory is faster than disks.

/LAZY stands for lazy writes. When a program needs to write data to the disk, the cache holds the data and writes it on the disk when the system is not busy. The system seems faster because programs do not have to wait for data to be written onto the disk. If you use lazy writes, you must run the Shutdown procedure before you turn off the computer; otherwise data that has not yet been written onto the disk will be lost.

CACHE works only on drives formatted with the High Performance File System. For FAT drives, use the DISKCACHE command.

CODEPAGE

Enables the computer to use, display, and print non-English language characters.

Syntax

CODEPAGE=primary,*secondary*

primary is a number that specifies the main national alphabet.

secondary is the number of another alphabet that you want to use in addition to the main national alphabet.

You can find the number for each alphabet in the on-line command reference, under the COUNTRY command.

Examples

To use the U.S. English alphabet and have the multinational alphabet available:

CODEPAGE=437,850

To use the Icelandic alphabet only:

CODEPAGE=861

Notes

OS/2 stores many different national character sets in *code pages*. You can load up to two pages through the CODEPAGE statement in CONFIG.SYS; only the first page is active, unless you switch to the other page with the CHCP command.

If you do not put a CODEPAGE statement in CONFIG.SYS, your keyboard uses an alphabet based on the COUNTRY statement, but your screen and printer use their built-in defaults.

The multinational alphabet, CODEPAGE=850, includes most of the accented letters used in European languages. Stick to the letters A-Z and numerals 0-9 for file and directory names so that people in other countries can use them.

COM and COM02

Enables you to use the communications ports for
mice, modems, and serial printers.

Syntax

DEVICE=path\COM.SYS

path is the location of the file COM.SYS. By default,
path is C:\OS2.

Example

To make the communications ports available, type
the following in CONFIG.SYS:

DEVICE=C:\OS2\COM.SYS

Notes

You must list COM.SYS after any driver that uses the
communications ports. A mouse driver, for example,
must come before COM.SYS in CONFIG.SYS.

Use COM02.SYS instead of COM.SYS if you have an
IBM PS/2 model 90 or 95.

COUNTRY

Customizes your system for the country you specify.

Syntax

COUNTRY=nnn,file

nnn is a three-digit number that indicates which
country's number-formatting conventions you want
OS/2 to use. The number is usually the same as the

telephone system's international dialing prefix for the country you specify. You can find these numbers in the on-line command reference, under the COUNTRY command.

file is the file that contains information for the country you specify. file is usually C:\OS2\SYSTEM\COUNTRY.SYS.

Example

To customize your system for the United Kingdom:

COUNTRY=044,C:\OS2\SYSTEM\COUNTRY.SYS

Notes

Dates, times, and numbers are formatted according to the custom of the country you specify. In France, one tenth of a second before February 1, 1993 looks like this:

31/01/1993 23:59:59,90

The SORT command works according to the order of the letters in the national alphabet of the country you specify.

DEVICE

Loads a device driver, which is a program that adds a function to the operating system.

Syntax

DEVICE=path\driver

path is the location of driver.

driver is the device driver file.

Example

To load the DOS ANSI driver:

DEVICE=C:\OS2\MDOS\ANSI.SYS

Notes

Device drivers are special programs that become part of OS/2 when you load them. Think of them as optional parts of OS/2. If you want to run DOS, for example, you need to load DOS.SYS. If you do not need DOS support, you do not need to load DOS.SYS. You can save memory by only loading the device drivers you need.

Mouse support is another example. OS/2 includes device drivers for six different types of mice, but you probably have only one mouse. It would waste memory to build in support for the other five types.

DEVICEHIGH

DOS Only

Loads a DOS device driver into upper memory, leaving more low memory available to run programs.

Syntax

DEVICEHIGH=path\driver

path is the location of driver.

driver is the device driver file.

Example

To load the ANSI driver into upper memory:

DEVICEHIGH=C:\OS2\MDOS\ANSI.SYS

Notes

DOS programs run in low memory (the first 640K).
DOS device drivers normally load in low memory,
which leaves less space to run programs. When you
load device drivers in upper memory (from 640K to
1024K), you keep more low memory free, giving DOS
programs more space.

If you do not have enough upper memory to load
the driver, OS/2 loads it in low memory.

DEVINFO (Keyboard)

Sets the keyboard layout for the country you
specify.

Syntax

DEVINFO=KBD,layout,path\KEYBOARD.DCP

layout is an abbreviation for your country, such as
US for United States. You can find these abbrevia-
tions in the on-line command reference.

path is the location of the file KEYBOARD.DCP.
This file specifies which characters map to each
keypress. By default, path is C:\OS2.

Example

To use the US keyboard:

DEVINFO=KBD,US,C:\OS2\KEYBOARD.DCP

DEVINFO (Printer)

Tells the printer object the country whose national characters it should use.

Syntax

DEVINFO=printer,model,*ROM=(font,0)*

printer is LPT1, LPT2, or LPT3.

model is 4201 for the IBM Proprinter, or 5202 for the IBM Quietwriter. Other manufacturers' printers also may have National Language Support. Refer to your printer's manual.

font is a three-digit number you use to specify a national alphabet. You can find these numbers in the on-line command reference under the COUNTRY command.

Example

To set up an IBM Proprinter, attached to the second printer port, for the United States:

DEVINFO=LPT2,4201,C:\OS2
\4201.DCP,ROM=(437,0)

DEVINFO (Screen)

Tells OS/2 what kind of screen you have.

Syntax

DEVINFO=SCR,type,path\VIOTBL.DCP

type is CGA, EGA, VGA, or BGA, depending on the kind of screen you have. BGA is the IBM 8514/A with memory expansion.

path is the location of the file VIOTBL.DCP, which tells what each character looks like. By default, path is C:\OS2.

Example

To tell OS/2 that you have a VGA monitor:

DEVINFO=SCR,VGA,C:\OS2\VIOTBL.DCP

Note

To configure OS/2 to work with your monitor, you also must set a couple of environment variables. OS/2's Install program performs this complicated task automatically. If you change your monitor, run Install to update the settings.

DISKCACHE

Makes your hard disk seem faster by keeping the data you use most frequently in memory.

Syntax

DISKCACHE=n,*LW, t, AC:x*

n is a number ranging from 64 to 14400 that tells OS/2 how many kilobytes of memory to set aside for remembering frequently used disk data.

LW (Lazy Write) tells the cache to delay writing data to the disk until the system is not quite so busy. *LW* is the default.

t, the cache threshold, is a number from 4 to 128 that expresses the number of disk sectors OS/2 should read or write at one time. A disk sector usually is 512 bytes. The default value of *t* is 4.

AC stands for Auto Check, and *x* is a drive letter. You can use this portion of the DISKCACHE command to tell OS/2 to check one or more drives at boot time. The check verifies the integrity of the directory and file structure on a drive by running the CHKDSK command with the /F option (see CHKDSK in the first section of the command reference). *x* can be any valid drive letter ranging from C to Z.

Examples

To set up a 256 kilobyte cache:

    DISKCACHE=256

To get even better performance with the same settings:

    DISKCACHE=256,LW,32

Notes

You probably use just a few programs and files at a time, which means that you are often reading the same parts of your hard disk over and over. When an application reads data from a disk, OS/2 looks in cache memory first for the data. If your application previously accessed the data, OS/2 can supply the data quickly from the cache without accessing the hard disk, which can make your hard disk seem much faster because memory is faster than disks. The cache acts as a staging area for disk data.

When the cache becomes full, data that you have not used in a while is discarded. If you work with files that are larger than the disk cache, data might be discarded before you need to use it again. To prevent this problem, you can limit the amount of data that is saved any particular time you read the disk by giving a value for *max*.

LW stands for Lazy Writing. When a program needs to write data to the disk, the cache holds the data and writes it on the disk when the system is not busy. The system seems faster because programs do not have to wait for data to be written onto the disk. If you use *LW*, you must run the Shutdown procedure before turning off the computer; otherwise, data that has not yet been written onto the disk is lost.

DISKCACHE works only on drives formatted with the FAT file system. For High Performance File System drives, use the CACHE command.

If your computer has less than 6 megabytes of physical memory, you should use a DISKCACHE size of 64 kilobytes. If you have more than 6 megabytes of physical memory, you may want to increase the cache size to 256 kilobytes. If you have an IBM PS/2 model 55sx, 65, 70, 80, 90, or 95, you should use a cache size of 64 kilobytes. These computers have a secondary cache inside the disk device driver.

DOS (Control memory)

DOS Only

Enables you to control how DOS uses memory.

Syntax

DOS=where,upper

where indicates whether DOS is loaded in high or low memory. **where** can be HIGH or LOW.

upper can be UMB or NOUMB. UMB enables DOS to run memory-resident programs in upper memory. NOUMB prevents DOS from running memory-resident programs in upper memory.

Example

To load DOS in high memory and enable it to run memory-resident programs in upper memory:

DOS=HIGH,UMB

Notes

DOS recognizes three different areas of memory. Low memory, from 0 to 640K, is where DOS programs, and DOS, usually run. With OS/2's special support, DOS programs also can run in upper memory, from 640K to 1024K. High memory is the area from 1024K to 1088K. OS/2 can move DOS to high memory.

The DOS operating system is really just a program that runs under OS/2. If you run DOS in low memory, you have less room to run DOS programs there. To avoid this problem, run DOS in high memory.

If you specify UMB, you can run DOS memory-resident programs in upper memory, using the LOADHIGH command. DOS=HIGH,UMB leaves the most lower memory free for applications.

DOS (Load DOS support)

DOS Only

Enables DOS sessions to work.

Syntax

DEVICE=path\DOS.SYS

path is the location of the file DOS.SYS. By default, path is C:\OS2.

Example

To load DOS support:

DEVICE=C:\OS2\DOS.SYS

Note

DOS sessions will not start unless you have this command in CONFIG.SYS.

DPATH

OS/2 Only

Tells OS/2 programs where to look for data files (but not executable program files).

Syntax

SET DPATH=dir1;*dir2;*...

dir1 is a directory, such as C:\MEMOS.

dir2 is another directory.

... means that you can specify more directories. Separate them from each other with semicolons.

Example

To tell OS/2 programs to look for data files in the directories C:\ and D:\DATA:

SET DPATH=C:\;D:\DATA

Notes

Data files that are in the current directory are always available to a program, even if you do not include the current directory in the DPATH statement.

The DOS APPEND command is similar to OS/2's DPATH. Unlike APPEND, DPATH works only with programs designed to use it, such as most commercial applications. Suppose that you have a file MEMO.TXT in a directory C:\MEMOS, and that directory is on your DPATH. A word processor in the C:\WORDPROC directory may be able to find the memo, but the OS/2 System Editor cannot find the memo unless you start it from the directory where the file is saved.

You normally set DPATH in CONFIG.SYS, but you also can set it in an OS/2 window. When you set a new DPATH, it replaces the old one.

EGA

DOS Only

Enables you to run DOS programs that control the Enhanced Graphics Adapter directly.

Syntax

> DEVICE=path\EGA.SYS

path is the location of the file EGA.SYS. By default, path is C:\OS2\MDOS.

Example

To load special EGA support, type the following in CONFIG.SYS:

> DEVICE=C:\OS2\MDOS\EGA.SYS

Note

If the mouse cursor leaves a trail on your screen, or you see strange characters in a DOS window, install this device driver. Some DOS programs, such as

games, control the EGA directly. These programs
work better if you load EGA.SYS. You may need EGA
support even if you have a VGA monitor because
some programs treat EGA and VGA alike. Don't load
EGA support unless you have a problem; it takes up
memory that your programs could use.

EXTDSKDD

Enables you to use an external disk drive, or specify
the type of disks used in an internal drive.

Syntax

DEVICE=path\EXTDSKDD.SYS /D:n *F:type*

path is the location of the file EXTDSKDD.SYS. By
default, path is C:\OS2.

n is the number of the disk drive. The first internal
drive is number zero. This drive is normally called
A, and the second drive (number one) is normally
called B. The first external drive is number two.

type is the kind of disk drive you have:

Type	Description	Capacity
0	5-1/4 inch double density	360 KB
1	5-1/4 inch high density	1.2 MB
2	3-1/2 inch double density	720 KB
3	3-1/2 inch high density	1.44 MB
4	3-1/2 inch ultra density	2.88 MB

Examples

To tell OS/2 that you have an external 5-1/4 inch
high density disk drive:

DEVICE=C:\OS2\EXTDSKDD.SYS /D:2 /F:1

To tell OS/2 to also use an internal 1.44M A drive for
720K disks:

DEVICE=C:\OS2\EXTDSKDD.SYS /D:0 /F:2

The drive is the same 1.44M drive when you call it A,
but a 720K drive when you call it B. If you have two
internal disk drives, the 720K drive is assigned a
higher letter, such as D.

Notes

You can use EXTDSKDD to tell an internal drive to
use disks of a different density. Be careful because
not every drive works this way. Even if it seems to
work, the disks you write on may not be readable on
a different computer. The value of *f* should be 0 or 1
for 5-1/4 inch drives, and 2, 3, or 4 for 3-1/2 inch
drives.

The internal drive still is available as drive A or as
drive B (if you have two internal drives).

EXTDSKDD creates a new drive letter. It uses the
first letter that was not already claimed. If you have
two internal disk drives A and B, and hard drives C
and D, for example, the new drive normally will be E.

EXTDSKDD has other parameters that you probably
will not need. If your external drive requires them,
follow the manufacturer's instructions. If the
instructions refer to DRIVER.SYS, use
EXTDSKDD.SYS instead.

FCBS

DOS Only

Supports File Control Blocks (FCBs), a method of
using files that was common in older DOS programs.

Syntax

FCBS=max,*protected*

max is the number of files, ranging from 0 to 255, that can be used at one time with the FCB method.

protected is the number of FCBs that will not be automatically closed when a program needs more FCBs than are available. It cannot be greater than max.

Examples

To give DOS ten FCBs and protect three from being closed:

FCBS=10,3

To give DOS 255 FCBs and tell it not to automatically recycle any of them if it runs out:

FCBS=255,255

Notes

You probably will not need to change the default, which is FCBS=16,16. Increase it to FCBS=255,255 if you have problems running DOS applications from the early 1980s.

If a program tries to open a file with an FCB, but all FCBs already are being used, the least recently used FCB is closed and given to the program. The file that was previously using the FCB is closed automatically, and any attempt to use it later causes an error. If all FCB's are protected, and they are all in use, a program that tries to open a file with an FCB will fail.

IFS

Enables you to use the High Performance File System (HPFS).

Syntax

IFS=path\HPFS.IFS */C:cache-size*
/AUTOCHECK:drives

path is the location of the file HPFS.IFS. By default,
path is C:\OS2.

cache-size is the number of kilobytes of memory
used as a disk cache. The default is 20% of total
memory.

drives is a list of disks that automatically is checked
for problems when you turn the computer on. Give
the letter of each drive; do not type a colon after the
letter.

Example

To start the High Performance File System with a
128K cache and check drives D and E for problems:

IFS=C:\OS2\HPFS.IFS */C:128*
/AUTOCHECK:DE

Notes

If you formatted one or more of your drives with
HPFS when you installed OS/2, the setup program
inserted an IFS statement in your CONFIG.SYS file.
You need this statement to use an HPFS drive.

HPFS has a disk cache to improve performance. You
probably use just a few programs and files at a time,
which means that you are often reading the same
parts of your hard disk over and over. A disk cache
saves whatever you have most recently read in
memory, and reads it directly from memory when
you need it again. It can make your hard disk seem
much faster because memory is faster than disks.
To use the HPFS cache, you need to use the */C*
switch and run the CACHE command.

The cache for HPFS drives, which you specify with the /C switch, is different from the cache for FAT drives, which you set up with the DISKCACHE command. Setting it too large can slow down your system because the memory the cache uses is not available for running programs. If you do not have enough room to run your programs, OS/2 swaps them to and from the disk, which negates the benefit of caching. A 128K cache usually is big enough.

The */AUTOCHECK* switch tells OS/2 to run the CHKDSK command when you turn the system on. CHKDSK detects and tries to fix problems with the file system. Use this switch with all HPFS drives; the safety CHKDSK provides is well worth the extra time it will take to start the system.

IOPL

OS/2 Only

Stands for I/O Privilege Level. Enables you to run programs that need to bypass OS/2 and work directly with hardware devices.

Syntax

IOPL=YES

YES means that all programs can access the hardware directly.

IOPL=NO

NO means that OS/2 will not allow computer programs to access the hardware directly.

IOPL=list

list gives the names of specific programs that are allowed to work directly with the hardware. Programs not listed cannot work directly with the hardware. Separate the names in the list with commas.

Examples

To prevent programs from working directly with the hardware:

IOPL=NO

To prevent any program except PROGRAM1 and PROGRAM2 from working directly with the hardware:

IOPL=PROGRAM1,PROGRAM2

Notes

OS/2 normally prevents programs from dealing directly with hardware such as adapter cards. One faulty program therefore cannot crash the whole system. Setting IOPL=NO offers the best protection against crashing the system.

Some programs have to work directly with the hardware to do things that OS/2 cannot do for them (such as giving instructions to a music interface adapter card). If you need to run such a program, specify its name in the list.

LIBPATH

OS/2 Only

Tells OS/2 programs where to look for Dynamic Link Libraries (DLLs).

Syntax

LIBPATH=dir1*;dir2;...*

dir1 is a directory, such as C:\LIBRARY. Use a period to indicate the current directory.

dir2 is another directory.

... means that you can specify more directories. Separate them from each other with semicolons.

Example

To tell OS/2 to look for DLLs first in the current directory, then in the directories C:\OS2\DLLS and D:\DLLS:

LIBPATH=.;C:\OS2\DLL;D:\DLL

The period following the equal sign means the current directory.

Notes

Many OS/2 applications put part of their program code in DLLs, which are program files with the extension DLL. To run these applications, OS/2 must know where to find their DLLs. Most applications come with an installation program that automatically adds the necessary LIBPATH to your CONFIG.SYS. Others may ask you to change it manually.

LIBPATH is similar to DPATH and PATH, but you can use LIBPATH only in CONFIG.SYS. You do not use the word SET when specifying LIBPATH. You should start LIBPATH with a period as in the example because OS/2 does not search the current directory for DLLs unless you include it.

MAXWAIT

OS/2 Only

Makes sure that no program thread is put on hold forever, even when the system is busy running other programs.

Syntax

MAXWAIT=n

n is the maximum number of seconds that a thread can be put on hold. The default is three seconds.

Example

To keep any thread from waiting on hold more than one second:

MAXWAIT=1

Notes

If you run several programs at a time, and a few of them grab most of the computer's attention, you still may want to be sure that even low-priority background programs make some progress. If a program has not received any attention for the number of seconds you set with MAXWAIT, OS/2 temporarily increases that program's priority.

The default, three seconds, usually is a good place to start. Try decreasing it to one if background programs run too slowly.

MEMMAN

OS/2 Only

Controls how OS/2 manages *virtual memory* (the memory OS/2 swaps in and out of the SWAPPER.DAT file in the C:\OS2\SYSTEM directory).

Syntax

MEMMAN=s,m,*PROTECT*

s is SWAP or NOSWAP.

m is MOVE or NOMOVE.

PROTECT enables the special programs in the C:\OS2\DLLS directory to allocate and use protected memory.

Example

To turn off virtual memory:

MEMMAN=NOSWAP,NOMOVE

Notes

OS/2 uses virtual memory to run more programs and use more data than can be stored in memory at once. OS/2 swaps segments of memory to disk when they are not being used and reads them back into memory when they are needed. Turn virtual memory on with SWAP, or turn it off with NOSWAP.

When a program runs, it allocates segments of memory and then releases them when it no longer needs the segments. Eventually, memory is fragmented into little pieces, slowing down the system. If you specify MOVE, OS/2 combines the fragmented pieces of memory, returning it to normal speed. Turn this feature off with NOMOVE.

The default, MEMMAN=SWAP,PROTECT, is the recommended setting. For some time-critical applications, however, you cannot afford even a fraction of a second for the computer to move or swap segments of memory. Specify NOMOVE and NOSWAP to increase the amount of memory needed to run the system.

MOUSE

Enables you to use a mouse or trackball.

Syntax

DEVICE=path\MOUSE.SYS TYPE=t *QSIZE=n*

path is the location of the file MOUSE.SYS. By default, path is C:\OS2.

t is the type of mouse you are using. Choose a mouse from the table in the "Notes" section.

n is a number ranging from 1 to 100 that tells OS/2 how many mouse actions to save when you work faster than the system can respond. Clicking on a menu item counts as one action. Dragging a file to the Print Manager also counts as one action. The default, 10, usually is enough.

Example

To tell OS/2 that you have a Visi-On mouse:

DEVICE=C:\OS2\MOUSE.SYS TYPE=VISION$

Notes

Look up your mouse in the following table:

Manufacturer/ model	Mouse type t	Special driver
IBM PS/2	PDIMOU$	PDIMOU02.SYS
Microsoft Bus	MSBUS$	(not needed)
Microsoft Serial	MSSER$	MSSER02.SYS
Microsoft Inport	MSINP$	(not needed)
PC Mouse Systems	PCMOU$	PCMOU02.SYS
Visi-On	VISION$	VISION02.SYS

If your mouse or trackball is not listed in the preceding table, a driver may be available from the manufacturer; otherwise, try installing it as one of the types shown.

To use a mouse with OS/2, you need to load several device drivers in CONFIG.SYS. OS/2 installation loads these device drivers, but you can make modifications by using the following steps.

Load POINTDD.SYS.

Load the special driver shown in the table, unless the table entry indicates that you do not need one.

Load MOUSE.SYS.

If you want to use the mouse in DOS sessions, load VMOUSE.SYS.

If you have a serial mouse, load COM.SYS.

For example, to install a Microsoft serial mouse on the second communications port and use it in DOS sessions:

DEVICE=C:\OS2\POINTDD.SYS

DEVICE=C:\OS2\MSSER02.SYS
   SERIAL=COM2

DEVICE=C:\OS2\MOUSE.SYS TYPE=MSSER$

DEVICE=C:\OS2\MDOS\VMOUSE.SYS

DEVICE=C:\OS2\COM.SYS

PATH

Tells OS/2 or DOS where to find programs.

Syntax

SET PATH=dir1*;dir2;...*

dir1 is a directory, such as C:\PROGRAMS.

dir2 is another directory.

... means that you can specify more directories. Separate them from each other with semicolons.

Examples

To tell OS/2 to look for program files in the directories C:\ and D:\UTILITY, enter this line in CONFIG.SYS, or type it in an OS/2 window:

    SET PATH=C:\;D:\UTILITY

To tell DOS to look for program files in the directories C:\ and D:\UTILITY, enter this line in AUTOEXEC.BAT, or type it in a DOS window:

    SET PATH=C:\;D:\UTILITY

Notes

You can run a program by using the CD command to change to the directory where you keep it. If that directory is on the PATH, however, you can run the program from any directory without specifying where the program is located on the disk.

You normally set the OS/2 PATH in CONFIG.SYS and the DOS PATH in AUTOEXEC.BAT. You also can use these commands in a DOS or OS/2 window. When you set a new PATH, the new PATH replaces the old one.

PAUSEONERROR

OS/2 Only

Tells OS/2 to stop for a moment if it cannot process a line in CONFIG.SYS correctly.

Syntax

> **PAUSEONERROR=YES**
>
> **PAUSEONERROR=NO**

Note

The default, YES, generally is the better choice. If OS/2 has a problem running a line in CONFIG.SYS, it displays an error message and waits until you press Enter. If the setting is NO, the error message appears, but it scrolls off the screen so quickly that you may not be able to read it.

PMDD

OS/2 Only

Enables Presentation Manager and its graphical user interface.

Syntax

> **DEVICE=path\PMDD.SYS**

path is the location of the file PMDD.SYS. By default, **path** is C:\OS2.

Example

To load PM:

> **DEVICE=C:\OS2\PMDD.SYS**

Note

OS/2 does not start unless this command is in CONFIG.SYS.

POINTDD

Draws the mouse pointer on-screen.

Syntax

DEVICE=path\POINTDD.SYS

path is the location of the file POINTDD.SYS.
By default, path is C:\OS2.

Example

To load mouse pointer support:

DEVICE=C:\OS2\POINTDD.SYS

Note

Installing a mouse requires other drivers as well. See
the explanation under the MOUSE command.

PRIORITY

OS/2 Only

Tells OS/2 whether it should vary the priority of
different threads that are running at the same time.

Syntax

PRIORITY=DYNAMIC

PRIORITY=ABSOLUTE

Notes

You normally should use **DYNAMIC** priority so that
OS/2 can vary the priority of threads, depending on

how active they are. Because a thread running in the foreground has a higher priority, the program with which you are currently working runs faster.

In the rare case that you need to run a program that sets its own thread priorities, use ABSOLUTE.

PROTECTONLY

OS/2 Only

Tells OS/2 whether you want to run DOS programs.

Syntax

PROTECTONLY=YES

PROTECTONLY=NO

Note

YES means you want to run only OS/2 programs. NO means you want to run DOS and OS/2 programs.

PROTSHELL

OS/2 Only

Loads OS/2's built-in command processor, CMD.EXE, or enables you to run a different command processor.

Syntax

PROTSHELL=startup

startup is the statement used to start the command processor. It includes the full path, the file's full name (including its extension), and various other parameters.

Examples

To use the built-in OS/2 command processor:

```
PROTSHELL=C:\OS2\PMSHELL.EXE
    C:\OS2\OS2.INI C:\OS2\OS2SYS.INI
    C:\OS2\CMD.EXE
```

Type these commands all on one line in CONFIG.SYS.

Note

The OS/2 command processor, also known as a shell, is the program that makes OS/2 full-screen and window sessions work. You may want to buy a different command processor to replace the shell that comes with OS/2. The new command processor will tell you which PROTSHELL command to use.

RMSIZE

DOS Only

Sets the amount of memory DOS can use.

Syntax

```
RMSIZE=n
```

n is the number of kilobytes of memory DOS can use, up to 640.

Example

To limit DOS to 512 kilobytes:

```
RMSIZE=512
```

Note

DOS normally can use up to 640K of memory. You usually should use **RMSIZE=640**, which is the default, because many programs require this amount. A smaller value will keep you from running some programs but will make more memory available to OS/2.

SET

Assigns values to variables in the environment.

Syntax

SET

SET var=value

var is the name of a variable in the environment.

value is what the name stands for.

Examples

To see the values of all environment variables, type this at the command line:

SET

To tell OS/2's on-line command reference that its files are stored in C:\OS2\BOOK:

SET BOOKSHELF=C:\OS2\BOOK

To tell OS/2 to look for its help messages in C:\OS2\HELP:

SET HELP=C:\OS2\HELP

To tell OS/2 to remember the commands you typed so that you can reuse them:

SET KEYS=ON

Note

The environment is a part of memory where values are assigned to certain names. The command processor and your applications use these names for various purposes. The PATH variable, for example, tells OS/2 where to find programs. DPATH, KEYS, and PROMPT also are environment variables.

SHELL

DOS Only

Loads OS/2's built-in DOS command processor COMMAND.COM, or enables you to run a different command processor.

Syntax

SHELL=startup

startup is the statement used to start the command processor. It includes the full path, the file's full name (including its extension), and any optional parameters.

Examples

To use the built-in DOS command processor:

SHELL=C:\OS2\MDOS\COMMAND.COM
C:\OS2\MDOS /P

To use JP Software's 4DOS shell instead, assuming that you have installed it in the D:\4DOS directory:

SHELL=D:\4DOS\4DOS.COM /P

Notes

The DOS command processor, also known as a shell, is the program that makes DOS sessions work. You may want to buy a different command processor that replaces the shell that comes with OS/2. The new command processor will tell you which SHELL command to use.

If you use a different shell, you must add a line to CONFIG.SYS that sets the COMSPEC variable to specify the full path and file name of the new shell. To use a different shell in the preceding 4DOS example, you must add the following line to CONFIG.SYS:

    SET COMSPEC=D:\4DOS\4DOS.COM

SWAPPATH

OS/2 Only

Tells OS/2 where to create the file SWAPPER.DAT. OS/2 uses this file as a memory overflow area so that you can run more programs than can fit in memory.

Syntax

    SWAPPATH=swapdir *minfree*

swapdir is a directory, such as C:\. The default is C:\OS2\SYSTEM.

minfree is a number ranging from 512 to 32767. It specifies the number of kilobytes of disk space that SWAPPER.DAT will leave free for your applications to use. If 2600K are free when you start OS/2, and *minfree* is 600, the swap file cannot grow larger than 2000K. The default for *minfree* is 512.

Example

To put the swap file in the \SWAP directory on drive D, and enable it to use all available space on D except for 1000K:

SWAPPATH=D:\SWAP 1000

Note

If you have a drive that is much faster or has much more free space than other drives, put the swap file on that drive. If you have sufficient disk space for a large swap file, you can run more programs and larger programs. The OS/2 installation process will set up a good *minfree* value for your system that you probably will not need to change, however.

THREADS

OS/2 Only

Sets the number of tasks OS/2 can perform at the same time.

Syntax

THREADS=n

n is the maximum number of threads, ranging from 32 to 4095.

Example

To allow up to 512 threads:

THREADS=512

Note

A thread is a part of a program that runs independently from the other parts of the program. A spreadsheet may create a thread when you tell it to save a file. This thread runs like a program in the background so that you can continue entering numbers in the spreadsheet without waiting for the file to be saved. The default is 64, but if you run several programs at once, try setting it to 256.

TIMESLICE

OS/2 Only

Sets upper and lower limits on the amount of time the computer spends on each thread (a running program or part of a running program).

Syntax

TIMESLICE *min,max*

min is a number between 32 and 65536. The computer must spend at least *min* thousandths of a second on each thread. The default is 32.

max is a number between 32 and 65535. The computer can spend no longer than *max* thousandths of a second on each thread. The default is whatever value is specified for *min*.

Examples

To set the minimum and maximum TIMESLICE to 32 and 500 thousandths of a second, respectively:

TIMESLICE=32,500

To set the maximum TIMESLICE to one second and use the default minimum value:

TIMESLICE=,1000

Notes

You should use 32 as the minimum value. A smaller value might cause OS/2 to spend too much time scheduling threads instead of allowing them to run.

If other threads are waiting to use the computer, OS/2 preempts the current thread after *min* milliseconds. No thread, however, gets more than *max* milliseconds of CPU time. If a thread exhausts a whole TIMESLICE, OS/2 gives that thread an extra measure of CPU time in its next turn. This way, OS/2 allocates the computer fairly to all applications, even those applications that require extra CPU time.

VCOM

DOS Only

Enables you to use the communications ports for DOS sessions.

Syntax

DEVICE=path\VCOM.SYS

path is the location of the file VCOM.SYS. By default, path is C:\OS2\MDOS.

Example

To make the communications ports available to DOS, type the following in CONFIG.SYS:

DEVICE=C:\OS2\MDOS\VCOM.SYS

Note

List VCOM.SYS *after* COM.SYS in CONFIG.SYS. Older versions of OS/2 used a program called SETCOM40 to provide communications support to DOS sessions, but you should not use SETCOM40 with OS/2 2.0.

VDISK

Makes a part of memory act like a fast electronic disk.

Syntax

DEVICE=path\VDISK.SYS **disk-size,sector-size,files**

path is the location of the file VDISK.SYS. By default, **path** is C:\OS2.

disk-size is a number from 16 to 4096 that gives the size of the virtual disk in kilobytes. The default is 64.

sector-size is the number of bytes in a sector. Just like a real disk, a virtual disk is divided into sectors. The value must be 128, 256, 512, or 1024. The default is 128 bytes.

files is a number ranging from 2 to 1024 that tells how many files you can put in the virtual disk's root directory. The default is 64.

Example

To create a 400K virtual disk with 256-byte sectors and a limit of 100 files in its root directory:

DEVICE=C:\OS2\VDISK.SYS 400,256,100

Notes

Virtual disks, also called RAM disks, act like real disk drives. Virtual disks are fast because they are part of the computer's memory, but they vanish when you turn the power off. The memory they take up cannot be used for other purposes, such as running programs. You probably will not want to use a virtual disk unless you have over eight megabytes of memory.

Try using a virtual disk to store files you read frequently, such as databases. You have to copy the database file to the RAM disk and then tell your database program to use the copy, which is safe if you only read the database to create reports. If you do any updates, however, you must copy the database back to your hard disk when you are finished. If you turn off the computer first, or the power goes off, you lose your updates.

VDISK creates a new drive letter. It uses the first letter that was not already claimed. If you have two hard drives C and D, for example, the virtual disk usually is E.

Add up the space required for all the files you want to put on the RAM disk and set *disk-size* a little larger in case your applications needs to write additional data to the files.

If you use the virtual disk for large files, a *sector-size* of 1024 gives the best performance. Because each file uses a whole number of sectors, however, a 100-byte file wastes 924 bytes. Use 128 for *sector-size* if your applications write many small files on the RAM disk.

Set *files* according to the number of files you want to use on the virtual disk. Add a few extra just in case. VDISK rounds *files* up to an even multiple of sixteen.

VEMM

DOS Only

Enables DOS applications to use expanded memory.

Syntax

DEVICE=path\VEMM.SYS *n*

path is the location of the file VEMM.SYS. By default, path is C:\OS2\MDOS.

n is the number of kilobytes of expanded memory available to each DOS session, ranging from 0 to 32768. The default is 4096, which is 4M.

Example

To give each DOS session up to one megabyte of expanded memory:

DEVICE=C:\OS2\VEMM.SYS 1024

Notes

Expanded memory, also called EMS or LIM 4.0, is a method for enabling DOS applications to use more than the usual 640K of memory. Most DOS spreadsheet programs use EMS so that you can work with large amounts of data.

You can override the amount of EMS available to each DOS application when you add it to a group by changing the value of EMS Memory Size under DOS Options.

To load expanded memory support without giving any expanded memory to DOS (unless you override it for a particular DOS session):

DEVICE=C:\OS2\VEMM.SYS 0

Put VEMM and VXMS at the end of CONFIG.SYS. VEMM and VXMS need to know which areas in memory other device drivers have already claimed so that they can make sure that they do not try to use those same areas.

VMOUSE

DOS Only

Enables you to use a mouse or trackball in DOS sessions.

Syntax

DEVICE=path\VMOUSE.SYS

path is the location of the file VMOUSE.SYS. By default, path is C:\OS2\MDOS.

Note

Installing a mouse requires other drivers as well. See the explanation under the MOUSE command.

PROGRAMMING WITH BATCH FILES

Batch files are to command line sessions what macros are to spreadsheets. Batch files store a series of commands that, when executed in combination, perform a useful task. You insert the commands in a file with a text editor, and then you type the file name at an OS/2 or DOS prompt when you want to run the sequence of commands. This procedure is easier and more foolproof than typing all the commands separately.

You easily can create a batch file with the Enhanced Editor. Type the commands you want to execute, one to a line, exactly as you would at the command line prompt. Save the file with any name you choose. The extension must be BAT (for a DOS batch file) or CMD (for one you want to run in an OS/2 session).

Creating a Sample Batch File

Suppose that you want to load UltraVision, a font enhancer from Personics, every time you run Borland's Turbo Pascal. Assume that UltraVision exists in the UV directory on your drive D, and the name of the program is UV.EXE. You want UV to use the 80-column, 50-line font. The Pascal compiler is called TURBO.EXE and is located in C:\TURBO. You can type this series of commands:

```
D:
CD \UV
UV 80X50
C:
CD \TURBO
TURBO
```

It is simpler, however, to type these commands into the editor once and save the file as C:\PASCAL.BAT. Now every time you type PASCAL at the DOS prompt, the commands run automatically. If you prefer to work from the Workplace Shell desktop, create a program object and type PASCAL.BAT on the first line of the Program page in the Settings notebook.

Batch files contain simple programming language statements along with DOS or OS/2 commands. The next few sections discuss some of the language statements and commands you can use in your batch file programs. You will learn how to make PASCAL.BAT do more work for you, and you will learn how to make PASCAL.BAT easier for you to read.

Inserting Comments with the REM Command

REM stands for remark. Your batch files are easier
to understand if you include remarks that explain
what they do. To insert a remark, begin a line with
the letters REM. Whatever you type on such a line is
not interpreted as a command; DOS or OS/2 skips
over it. In the preceding example, the line UV 80X50
is a little cryptic. To clarify your intention, insert the
following line:

> REM Load Ultravision's 80-column by 50-line
> font

Writing to the Screen with the ECHO Command

Remarks are visible only when you display a batch
file (in an editor, for example). You can display a
comment on-screen when you execute the batch file
by using ECHO instead of REM. They work the same
way, except that ECHO writes the remark to the
screen.

Passing Options to a Batch File

PASCAL.BAT would be even more useful if you could
specify the name of a program to load automatically
when Turbo Pascal starts. If you are not using the
batch file, you can load your mortgage program, for
example, by typing its name on the same line as the
compiler's name, as in the following:

> TURBO MORTGAGE.PAS

You need a way to pass information such as the
name of a file to your batch program. Options

provide the solution. Change the line that says TURBO to the following:

TURBO %1.PAS

The %1 stands for the first option you specify after the name of the batch file. The letters that follow, PAS, are tacked on, because Pascal source code files always end with that file extension. You can enter the following to load the mortgage program:

PASCAL MORTGAGE

You also can enter the following to load a program you wrote to generate random numbers for a lottery.

PASCAL LOTTERY

Whatever you type after the name of the batch file replaces the %1. Parameters %2 through %9 are available if you need to pass more than one piece of information.

Pausing the Batch Program

You can use a PAUSE statement in your batch file programs to temporarily suspend execution of the commands. The PAUSE statement tells OS/2 to display the message "Press any key to continue . . ." and wait for you to press a key. If you press Ctrl-C, you can stop the batch file program. Any other keystroke continues execution of the batch file statements.

Testing for Files with the IF EXIST Command

No programming language is complete without error-checking. For example, you may want to ensure that the file name passed as %1 exists before you try to run the program. If the file exists, load it into TURBO.EXE; if the file does not exist, you do not need to load the TURBO program. To express this programming specification in batch language, replace the last line of PASCAL.BAT with the following:

IF EXIST %1.PAS TURBO %1.PAS

Another form, IF NOT EXIST, executes the command at the end of the line only if the file you specify cannot be found in the current directory.

Changing the Flow with the GOTO Command

Most of the lines in a batch file are commands. These commands are executed in the order in which they appear. Sometimes you want to change the flow of execution, however. PASCAL.BAT would be easier to use, for example, if it told you whether or not the IF EXIST test finds the file you gave as an option. If it finds the file, enter the following line.

ECHO Loading %1.PAS into TURBO...
    TURBO %1.PAS

On the other hand, if it does not find the file, you want to display the following message:

ECHO *
ECHO * Sorry, there is no file named %1.PAS *
ECHO *

The GOTO command provides the answer. GOTO tells DOS to go to a line other than the next one you specify. Mark the line you want to go to with a name that makes sense to you, preceded by a colon. For example, you can enter :END as the last line in a batch file so that when you say GOTO END, your batch program jumps to the end of the file. Notice that you do not use the colon on the GOTO line; the colon is used only to mark the destination of the GOTO command.

When you put all this information together, your finished PASCAL.BAT looks like the following.

```
D:
CD\UV
ECHO Load Ultravision's 80 column by 50 line
    font
UV 80X50
C:
CD\TURBO
REM See whether %1.pas exists; jump to :FOUND
    if it does
IF EXIST %1.PAS GOTO FOUND
REM
REM If execution continues with this line,
REM the file did not exist,
REM so display this error message:
REM
ECHO * * * * * * * * * * * * * * * * * * *
ECHO * Sorry, there is no file named %1.PAS *
ECHO * * * * * * * * * * * * * * * * * * *
REM
REM Skip the lines that load TURBO.PAS
GOTO END
REM
:FOUND
REM If execution reaches this line,
REM the file exists, so load TURBO
REM
ECHO Loading %1.PAS into TURBO...
TURBO %1.PAS
REM
:END
```

This program may look long, but consider the following:

■ Thirteen of the 28 lines in this file are remarks. The file would be much shorter without them, but it would be harder to understand. Six of the remarks are blank; you use them to separate sections for legibility.

■ Five of the lines are ECHO statements, which give useful information while the program is running. Notice that the text on the ECHO and REM lines is in lowercase, which makes the other lines stand out.

■ Only six lines are DOS commands. The remaining four control the flow of execution in the batch file.

Cleaning the Display with the ECHO OFF Command

When DOS executes PASCAL.BAT, each line is displayed on-screen, which helps you detect mistakes when you are designing a batch program. When you are satisfied with the final program, however, you don't want every single line echoed to the screen. Turn this feature off by entering the following line at the top of the file:

ECHO OFF

This command tells DOS to run the batch file silently. Only lines beginning with ECHO are displayed.

Using Startup Batch Files that Run Automatically

Two batch files that run every time you start a command line session are AUTOEXEC.BAT and STARTUP.CMD. AUTOEXEC.BAT executes when you open a DOS session, and STARTUP.CMD runs at the beginning of each OS/2 session. Use these files for commands that you always want to run. If you want UltraVision loaded at the beginning of every DOS session, for example, insert the appropriate lines in AUTOEXEC.BAT.

Halting a Batch Program

When you find an error in a batch file you are developing, you may need to stop it quickly. For example, consider the following program:

```
:START
GOTO START
```

This program will run forever. You can terminate a batch program at any time by pressing Ctrl-Break, however.

For the advanced programmer, OS/2 includes REXX, a complete programming language similar to batch programming but much more extensive. REXX has its own manual and on-line help system.

OS/2 2.0 ENHANCED EDITOR

The Enhanced Editor is a tool you use to create, view, and modify text files. The OS/2 installation process puts the Enhanced Editor in the Productivity Folder, which is in the OS/2 System Folder. The executable file is EPM.EXE and exists in the \OS2\APPS directory.

To start the editor, double-click on the Enhanced Editor icon in the Productivity Folder or type EPM at an OS/2 full-screen or windowed command-line prompt.

To exit the editor, press Alt-F4 or use the quit option in the File menu.

With the Enhanced Editor, you can do the following:

- Copy and rearrange lines and paragraphs
- Scan files for a word or phrase

■ Search for and replace one word or phrase with another

■ Move and copy text between files

■ Undo any or all changes you made

■ Use different fonts and colors

■ Edit several files at once

■ Customize the appearance of the editor

Enhanced Editor Keystroke Guide

Keystroke	Function
F1	Get help
F2	Save and continue
F3	Quit without saving
F4	Save and quit
F5	Open file
F6	Show draw options
F7	Change filename
F8	Edit new file
F9	Undo current line
F10	Activate menu
Alt-F1	Insert line-drawing characters
Alt-F4	Close window
Alt-F5	Restore window
Alt-F7	Move
Alt-F8	Size
Alt-F9	Minimize
Alt-F10	Maximize

Keystroke	Function
Shift-F2	Scroll right
Shift-F3	Scroll up
Shift-F4	Scroll down
Shift-F5	Scroll to put the current line in the center of the screen
Ctrl-F1	Uppercase word
Ctrl-F2	Lowercase word
Ctrl-F3	Uppercase selection
Ctrl-F4	Lowercase selection
Ctrl-F5	Cursor to beginning of word
Ctrl-F6	Cursor to last character of word

Enhanced Editor Cursor Movement Keystrokes

Keystroke	Function
Left arrow	Left one letter
Ctrl-Left	Left one word
Right arrow	Right one letter
Ctrl-Right	Right one word
Up arrow	Up one line
Down arrow	Down one line
PgUp	Up one page
Ctrl-PgUp	Top of page
PgDn	Down one page
Ctrl-PgDn	Bottom of page

Keystroke	Function
Home	Beginning of line
Ctrl-Home	Beginning of file
End	End of line
Ctrl-End	End of file

Marking, Cutting, Copying, Pasting

To mark a block of text, move the mouse cursor to the beginning of the block. Hold down the left button and move the mouse cursor to the end of the block. When you move the mouse, the block is highlighted. Release the button when you are finished. With the keystrokes in the following list, you can remove or insert blocks in the editor, just like cutting and pasting paper documents.

Cutting. Pressing Shift-Del removes a marked block of text from the file and places it in a temporary holding area called the clipboard. You can insert the block elsewhere in the document by using the Paste command.

Copying. Pressing Ctrl-Ins copies a block of text to the clipboard. Copying a block works like the Cut command except that it does not delete the original block.

Pasting. To paste a block of text from the clipboard into a document, move the cursor where you want to insert the block and press Shift-Ins. The block appears at the new location and the surrounding text is pushed down to make room. Pasting does not clear the clipboard; you can press Ctrl-Ins repeatedly to insert several copies of the text.

File Menu

New empties out all the text in the current editor window and gives you a blank screen to begin a new file.

Open Untitled starts up a new, empty editor window. The new window overlaps the original one.

Open starts up a new editor window and loads a file.

Import text file inserts the contents of a text file at the current cursor position of the file you are editing.

Rename enables you to change the name of the current file.

Save writes the current file to disk.

Save as is a combination of Rename and Save.

Save and quit combines the functions of Save and Quit.

Quit closes the current window. If the current window is the only open EPM window, Quit also closes the editor.

Print file enables you to print a copy of your file.

Edit Menu

Undo line restores an entire line to its state before you began making changes.

Undo... Undo presents you with a slider bar. To undo your changes one at a time, press the left-arrow key repeatedly. Use the right-arrow key to reapply each change in order. You also can drag the slider with the mouse. Move the mouse pointer to the slider, hold down the left button, and move the slider to the left or right by moving the mouse.

Copy places marked (selected) text in the clipboard without removing it from the file you are editing.

Cut deletes marked (selected) text and places the text in the clipboard.

Paste inserts clipboard text at the current cursor location.

Paste lines inserts lines of clipboard text at the current cursor location.

Paste block inserts a marked block of text at the current cursor location.

Style enables you to set various color and font preferences.

Copy mark copies marked text to the current cursor location.

Move mark moves marked text to the current cursor location.

Overlay mark overwrites text at the current cursor location with marked text.

Adjust mark copies marked text to the current cursor location and fills the original text position with blanks.

Unmark unmarks any marked text.

Delete mark deletes marked text.

Print mark... prints marked text.

Search Menu

Search... enables you to find words and phrases in the file.

Find next finds the next occurence of the word or phrase for which you are looking.

Change next performs the next change action during a search-and-replace operation.

Bookmarks enables you to set, remove, list, and go to bookmarks you set in the file.

Options Menu

List ring lists the names of the files you're editing (if you are editing more than one file in ring fashion and have enabled ring editing with the preferences menu).

Preferences enables you to change settings note-book entries (described later in this section) and set advanced marking, stream editing, ring enabled, and stack commands options.

Autosave displays a window in which you can tell the Enhanced Editor how often to automatically save the file you are editing.

Messages shows you a list of informational, error, and warning messages displayed by the Enhanced Editor.

Frame controls enables you to customize the appearance of the Enhanced Editor screen. You can toggle the display of the status line, message line, scrollbars, rotate buttons, and prompting. You can choose whether you want the Editor to display information at the top of the screen or bottom.

Save options preserves your options settings so that they are in effect the next time you use the Enhanced Editor.

Command Menu

Command dialog activates an Enhanced Editor command line at which you can enter editor com-mands or OS/2 commands.

Halt command enables you to interrupt the execu-tion of a command that is in progress.

Settings Notebook

After changing options on one or more notebook pages, press one of the following buttons at the bottom of the notebook page:

Set saves the options you have selected as your personal default for all files.

Apply uses the selected options only on the current file. The options are not saved when you quit the editor.

Defaults restores the original settings, clearing any settings you saved with Set.

Setting Tab Stops

Choose Tabs and type a single number in the input field on this screen to tell EPM how many spaces to insert when you press the Tab key. The default setting of eight spaces usually is appropriate. You can use tab stops to create table columns; this method works best with a monospaced font, where all characters are the same width. If you want to line text up in columns 10, 15, and 28, for example, type those three numbers on this settings notebook page.

Setting Margins

You can use this page of the notebook to set the left and right margins for your file. The paragraph margin controls the number of spaces that the first line of each paragraph should be indented.

Unlike word processors, the Enhanced Editor works with lines rather than paragraphs. If you use it to type memos, however, you need a way to reformat each paragraph to fit the margins you set. You can move the cursor to the character following the one where you want the reformatting to begin and press Alt-P to cause the Editor to reflow the words in the paragraph according to your current margin settings.

Choosing Colors and Fonts

You can use the Colors and Fonts settings notebook pages to specify the colors and fonts you prefer to see on the Enhanced Editor screen.

Saving Files Automatically

You can use the settings on the Autosave page to tell the Enhanced Editor to automatically save your editing changes. By default, the Enhanced Editor saves a file after every 100 changes. This setting is generally satisfactory. To turn off this feature, set the number to zero.

OS/2 2.0 MESSAGES

The message files that OS/2 uses are large. A printout of all the messages would be much longer than this book. You can ask OS/2 to retrieve the contents of its message files for any message, however. To ask OS/2 for an explanation and suggested course of action for a particular error message, you can type the following:

HELP <message number>

If you see the message SYS0015: The system cannot find the drive specified, for example, you can type **HELP 15**. OS/2 displays the following message:

> EXPLANATION: One of the following has occurred:
>
> 1. The drive specified does not exist.
>
> 2. The drive letter is incorrect.
>
> 3. You are trying to RESTORE to a redirected drive.
>
> ACTION: For situations 1 and 2 above, retry the command by using the correct drive letter. For situation 3, you are not allowed to RESTORE to a redirected drive.

If you see the message The system is stopped. Record the location number of the error and contact your service representative displayed by OS/2, usually on a screen containing another message telling you The system detected an internal processing error, you cannot ask OS/2 for further information about the error. You must reboot your computer.

OS/2 2.0 COMMAND SURVIVAL GUIDE

Commands that help you work with your files

ATTRIB	Shows or changes a file's read-only and archive attributes.
BACKUP	Backs up a hard disk to floppy disks.
COMP	Compares files.

COPY	Copies or combines files.
DEL	Erases files.
ERASE	Erases files.
FIND	Searches for text in files.
MORE	Displays a file one screen at a time.
MOVE	Moves files from one directory to another on the same drive.
PRINT	Prints files.
RECOVER	Partially salvages files from a disk with bad sectors.
REN or RENAME	Changes a file's name.
REPLACE	Selectively copies files.
RESTORE	Retrieves files from a backup.
SORT	Sorts the lines in a file alphabetically.
TYPE	Displays a file on-screen.
UNPACK	Restores compressed files on an OS/2 distribution floppy disk to their normal, uncompressed form.
VERIFY	Checks that data is written to a disk.
XCOPY	Copies directories or groups of files.

Commands that help you work with your directories

APPEND	Tells DOS programs where to find data files.
CD or CHDIR	Shows or changes the current directory of a disk drive.
DIR	Lists the files in a directory.
MD or MKDIR	Creates a directory.
RD or RMDIR	Removes a directory.
TREE	Displays all directories on a disk.

Commands that help you prepare and maintain disks and diskettes

CACHE	Controls the disk cache on HPFS drives.
CHKDSK	Analyzes a disk and gives you a report. Fixes disk problems.
DISKCOMP	Determines whether one floppy disk is an exact copy of another.
DISKCOPY	Duplicates a floppy disk.
FDISK or FDISKPM	Manages hard disk partitions.
FORMAT	Prepares a disk for use and reports any defects.
LABEL	Gives a name to a disk.
MAKEINI	Recovers from a Corrupt OS2.INI error.
VOL	Displays a disk's label and serial number.

The following commands work with the CONFIG.SYS commands CODEPAGE, COUNTRY, and DEVINFO.

Commands that support national languages

CHCP	Switches between national alphabets.
GRAFTABL	Enables DOS programs to display line-drawing and national language characters on a CGA monitor in graphics mode.
KEYB	Tells the keyboard which national alphabet you want to use.

Commands that give you information about your system or enable you to change how it works

ANSI	Enables you to run OS/2 programs that require special support for the screen or keyboard.
ASSIGN	Redirects requests for disk operations on one drive to a different drive.
BOOT	Loads a different operating system.
CLS	Clears the screen.
CMD	Starts a new copy of the OS/2 command processor.
COMMAND	Starts a new copy of the DOS command processor.
DATE	Displays or sets the date.
DETACH	Runs a noninteractive program in the background.
EXIT	Terminates the current command processor.
HELP	Explains how to use a command, or what an error message means.
JOIN	Tells DOS to join a disk drive to a directory on another drive.
KEYS	Controls command recall and editing.
MODE	Controls the communications port, screen mode, or parallel printer.
PROMPT	Sets the string of characters that is displayed at the command line.
SPOOL	Redirects a file that you send to one printer, so that it comes out on a different printer.

START	Runs a program automatically.
SUBST	Establishes an alias consisting of a drive letter for a path.
TIME	Displays or sets the time.
VER	Displays the version of OS/2 you are using.
VIEW	Looks up a topic in an on-line help document.

You can place the following commands in the CONFIG.SYS file that OS/2 reads each time it starts. CONFIG.SYS statements give information that OS/2 needs to control the computer and run programs. With the exception of the ANSI, PROMPT, SET, and PATH statements, you do not type CONFIG.SYS statements at a command line prompt.

Configuration commands

ANSI	Enables you to run those OS/2 programs that require special support for the screen or keyboard.
AUTOFAIL	Gives you a choice in dealing with certain hardware errors.
BREAK	Controls how quickly DOS programs stop when you interrupt them by pressing Ctrl-Break.
BUFFERS	Sets aside a part of memory that OS/2 uses to hold disk data.
CODEPAGE	Enables the computer to use, display, and print non-English language characters.
COM	Enables you to use the communications ports for mice, modems, and serial printers.

COUNTRY	Customizes your system for the country you specify.
DEVICE	Loads a device driver, which is a program that adds a function to the operating system.
DEVICEHIGH	Loads a DOS device driver into upper memory, leaving more low memory available to run programs.
DEVINFO	Sets the keyboard, printer, and screen for the country you specify.
DISKCACHE	Makes your hard disk seem faster by keeping the data you use most frequently in memory.
DOS	Enables you to run DOS sessions and control the use of memory.
DPATH	Tells OS/2 programs where to look for data files.
EGA	Enables you to run DOS programs that control the Enhanced Graphics Adapter directly.
EXTDSKDD	Enables you to use an external disk drive, or specify the type of disks used in an internal drive.
FCBS	Supports File Control Blocks, a method of using files that was common in older DOS programs.
IFS	Enables you to use the High Performance File System.
IOPL	Enables you to run programs that need to bypass OS/2 and work directly with hardware devices.
LIBPATH	Tells OS/2 programs where to look for Dynamic Link Libraries.
LOADHIGH	Enables you to load DOS memory-resident programs into upper memory.

MAXWAIT	Makes sure that no program thread is put on hold forever, even when the system is busy running other programs.
MEMMAN	Controls how OS/2 manages virtual memory.
MOUSE	Enables you to use a mouse or trackball.
PATH	Tells OS/2 or DOS where to find programs.
PAUSEONERROR	Tells OS/2 to stop for a moment if it cannot process a line in CONFIG.SYS correctly.
PMDD	Enables Presentation Manager and its graphical user interface.
POINTDD	Draws the mouse pointer on-screen.
PRIORITY	Tells OS/2 whether it should juggle the priority of different threads that are running at the same time.
PROTECTONLY	Tells OS/2 whether you want to run DOS programs.
PROTSHELL	Loads OS/2's built-in command processor CMD.EXE, or enables you to run a different command processor.
RMSIZE	Sets the amount of memory DOS can use.
SET	Assigns values to variables in the environment.
SHELL	Loads OS/2's built-in DOS command processor COMMAND.COM, or enables you to run a different one.
SWAPPATH	Tells OS/2 where to create the file SWAPPER.DAT.

THREADS	Sets the number of tasks OS/2 can perform at the same time.
TIMESLICE	Sets upper and lower limits on the amount of time the computer spends on each thread.
VCOM	Enables you to use the communications ports for DOS sessions.
VDISK	Makes a part of memory act like a fast electronic disk.
VEMM	Enables DOS applications to use expanded memory.
VMOUSE	Enables you to use a mouse or trackball in DOS sessions.

Other commands

Two groups of commands are not included here. Because this book does not discuss the details of REXX or advanced batch file programming, the following batch commands are not covered:

- CALL
- ENDLOCAL
- EXTPROC
- FOR
- PMREXX
- SETLOCAL
- SHIFT

The following commands are used only by technical service personnel:

- CREATEDD
- LOG

- PATCH
- PSTAT
- SYSLEVEL
- SYSLOG
- TRACE
- TRACEBUF
- TRACEFMT

WORKPLACE SHELL SURVIVAL GUIDE

This section contains keyboard shortcuts and mouse operations for various Workplace Shell tasks. In this section, "mouse button 2" refers to the right mouse button unless you have changed your mouse settings.

Workplace Shell Task	Do These Steps
Close	Double-click on the a window Menu button in the upper left corner of the window.
Close	Point the mouse at an a window object and press mouse or notebook button 2 once. Click on the Close option.
Copy	Position the mouse pointer an object on the object you want to copy. Hold the Ctrl key while you use mouse button 2 to drag the object to a new location.

Workplace Shell Task	Do These Steps
Create a shadow of an object	Position the mouse pointer on the object to be copied. Hold the Ctrl and Shift keys while you use mouse button 2 to drag the object to a new location.
Delete an object	Use mouse button 2 to drag and drop the object on the shredder.
Display an object's System menu	Position the mouse pointer on the object and click the right mouse button.
Display the window list	Position the mouse pointer on an empty place on the desktop. Press the left and right mouse buttons at the same time.
Drag-and-drop	Position the mouse pointer on the object. Press and hold mouse button 2 while you move the mouse pointer to the position where you want the object located. Release button 2 when you have moved the object to its new location.
Dual-boot DOS	Double-click the OS/2 System folder, double-click the Command Prompts folder, and then double-click the Dual Boot icon.
Find an object	Display a folder's popup menu. Choose the Find option.
Maximize a window	Double-click the left mouse button on the window title bar or click once with the left mouse button on the Maximize button (the button with a large square in the upper right corner of the window).

Workplace Shell Task	Do These Steps
Minimize a window	With the left mouse button, click once on the Minimize button (the button with a small square, to the left of the Maximize button).
Move a window	Click either mouse button on the window's title bar and move the mouse while holding the button down. Release the mouse button.
Open an object	Position the mouse pointer on the object and press button 1 twice, in rapid succession (double-click).
Open settings notebook	Position the mouse pointer on the object and press button 2 once. Click the mouse on the arrow to the right of the Open menu option. Click on the Settings option.
Open workplace shell's system menu	Click the right mouse button on any blank spot on the desktop. The keyboard equivalent consists of the following six steps:
	1. Pop up the Window List.
	2. Select the Desktop.
	3. Press Enter.
	4. Press the spacebar to unselect the current icon.
	5. Hold down Shift while you press F10.
	6. Release both keys.
Print an object	Drag and drop the object on the appropriate printer object.

Workplace Shell Task	Do These Steps
Resize a window	Move the mouse pointer to any edge or corner of the window. When the mouse pointer changes to a double arrow, hold down either mouse button and move the mouse to resize the window. Release the button.
Restore a window to its original size	Double-click the title bar or click on the Restore button—a medium-size square between two vertical lines.
See an object's popup menu	Position the mouse pointer on the object and press button 2 once.
See the desktop's popup menu	Position the mouse pointer on an empty place on the desktop and press button 2 once.
Select an object	Position the mouse pointer on the object and press button 1 once.
Shut down	Position the mouse pointer on an empty place on the desktop and press button 2 once. Click on the Shutdown option. Confirm the operation and then wait for OS/2 to tell you it is safe to reboot or turn off your computer.
Start a program object	Move the mouse pointer to the object and double-click with the left mouse button.

Workplace shell keyboard shortcuts

Keystroke	Function
Alt-Esc	Switch to the next open window or full-screen session.
Alt-Home	Switch a DOS program between window and full screen.
Ctrl-Alt-Del	Restart the operating system.
Ctrl-Esc	Display the Window List.
Alt-PgDn	In a notebook, move cursor to the next page.
Alt-PgUp	In a notebook, move cursor to the preceding page.
F1	Display help for the active window.
F5	Refresh contents of the active window.
F6	Move cursor from one window pane to another when using an application's split window feature.
F10	Move the cursor to or from the menu bar.
Alt-F4	Close the active window.
Alt-F5	Restore window to its previous size.

Keystroke	Function
Alt-F6	Move the cursor between associated windows, such as the Master Help Index and its currently displayed topic.
Alt-F7	Move the active window.
Alt-F8	Size the active window or selected object.
Alt-F9	Minimize, hide, or remove the active window from the screen.
Alt-F10	Maximize window.
Shift-Esc or Alt-Spacebar	Switch to or from the title-bar icon.
Shift-F8	Start or stop selecting more than one object while using the space bar to select an object.
Shift-F10	Display pop-up menu for the active object.

INDEX